Riley Knight is the host of *Half-Arsed History*, a weekly podcast highlighting absurd and entertaining stories from history. Born in Melbourne, Victoria, Riley became a primary school teacher after finishing his mostly useless Arts degree, and began *Half-Arsed History* as a hobby while teaching grade three. The podcast has only grown since then, with millions of downloads across the world, live shows across Australia, and now its very own book.

After spending almost a decade living in Europe, Riley now lives on the Sunshine Coast in Queensland, and consistently produces three episodes of *Half-Arsed History* every week (except when the cricket is on, at which time he produces them inconsistently). He enjoys reading, long-distance running, and collecting little historical artefacts.

HISTORY'S STRANGEST DEATHS

A Half-Arsed History Book

RILEY KNIGHT

First published in 2025

Allen & Unwin
Cammeraygal Country
83 Alexander Street
Crows Nest NSW 2065
Australia
Phone: (61 2) 8425 0100
Email: info@allenandunwin.com
Web: www.allenandunwin.com

Allen & Unwin acknowledges the Traditional Owners of the Country on which we live and work. We pay our respects to all Aboriginal and Torres Strait Islander Elders, past and present.

EU Authorised Representative: Easy Access System Europe, Mustamäe tee 50, 10621 Tallinn, Estonia, gpsr.requests@easproject.com

A catalogue record for this book is available from the National Library of Australia

ISBN 978 1 76147 258 9

Set in 12/19 pt Garamond Premier Pro by Midland Typesetters, Australia
Printed and bound in Australia by the Opus Group

10 9 8 7 6 5

The paper in this book is FSC® certified. FSC® promotes environmentally responsible, socially beneficial and economically viable management of the world's forests.

For Mum and Dad

You do not know where death awaits you; so be ready for it everywhere.

Seneca the Younger

Contents

Introduction

Dying is a favourite pastime of ours. Throughout the broad sweep of human history, most people have tried it at least once, and unlike so many widespread and once-fashionable mainstays that have fallen by the wayside over the years—stone tools, powdered wigs, and scurvy, for example—death has shown considerable staying power.

As it happens, participation rates are at an all-time high: the latest figures confirm that more people have died now than at any other point in history. Every year, more and more of us are giving it a go, and remarkably, not a single person has come back with any complaints. Despite us doing it for thousands of years, we still don't seem to be tired of dying; according to the numbers, death continues to be one of the most popular human activities to date. It certainly has proven to have a lot more longevity than we do, in any case.

Not all deaths are created equal, however. Many people are supremely unimaginative when it comes to how they die: they unashamedly embrace tired old clichés by doing things such as dying peacefully in their sleep, surrounded by loved ones. How unadventurous! Even the leading cause of death worldwide, ischaemic heart disease, might seem very exciting at first glance thanks to such scientific-sounding terminology, but just refers to when someone gets old enough that their ticker gives up. Despite our limitless creativity in life, the overwhelming majority of those who have died throughout history have done so in rigidly conventional ways.

A select few people, however, have instead made their mark in the history books by exiting this world in thrillingly unconventional ways. From a nobleman being assassinated while on the toilet to a pair of kings who died after whacking their heads on a pair of doorframes; from a soldier being beaten to death with his own wooden leg to a lawyer shooting himself to prove a legal point, history is full of examples of people who did not give the Grim Reaper just another quiet day at the office. Instead, they're remembered for going out in some of the strangest circumstances you could possibly imagine.

In the fullness of time, there's a very good chance that you, dear reader, will give death a go at some point or another. You might consider this to be anything from an inescapable inconvenience to an unknowable source of existential dread; whatever the case, death isn't something to worry about too much. After all, dying isn't the end of the world—it's just the end of yours.

All the same, that's not to say you should be in a rush, as there's plenty of time for you to get around to dying eventually. In the meantime, sit back and enjoy the ride, and be sure to make the most of all of the wonderful little things that make life worth living: having a nice club sandwich with chips for lunch, ruthlessly teasing a mate when they pronounce a word slightly incorrectly, or, best of all, reading tinpot history books about strange deaths.

But when your time does come, if you're lucky—or, to be honest, if you're unlucky—you might die in a way that is strange, amusing, entertaining or ridiculous. If so, you could be the one appearing in the next tinpot history book about strange deaths; although, sadly, you won't be around to read it.

I

Duke Jing of Jin

Died after Falling into a Toilet, 581 BCE

Between 599 and 581 BCE, the ancient Chinese state of Jin was ruled by a man named Duke Jing. Located in the region north of the modern Chinese city of Zhengzhou, Jin was a very powerful state during the Spring and Autumn Period of ancient Chinese history, which lasted from around 770 to 476 BCE.

Duke Jing of Jin did his best as a ruler. He's certainly not the most remarkable or successful leader from ancient Chinese history, but he's far from the worst. He went about scrapping with other regional powers, winning some battles, losing others, ultimately leaving the realm more or less as he found it. Duke Jing of Jin was like a pet goldfish: he did his job in his little part of the world in a thoroughly unspectacular fashion, and then after he died he ended up at the bottom of a toilet.

In 581 BCE, after eighteen years as duke, Jing fell ill and decided to retire. He abdicated in favour of his son, who became Duke Li of Jin, and settled down to get really into crosswords, or gardening, or whatever the ancient Chinese equivalent of pickleball was. He didn't have much of a chance to do this, however, because he was dead within a short time of handing over the reins, as related by an ancient Chinese narrative history text called the *Zuo Zhuan*.

According to the *Zuo Zhuan*, ex-Duke Jing was plagued by terrible nightmares after his retirement. He kept dreaming that an evil spirit was coming for him, and so he consulted a *wu*—a type of shaman—to receive guidance as to what he should do. Unfortunately for him, the *wu's* assessment wasn't exactly optimistic: she foresaw that the duke wouldn't live long enough to 'eat the new wheat'. In other words, Jing would be dead before the next harvest. As you might imagine, Jing was none too pleased about this dire prediction.

His bad dreams intensified as he convinced himself that his end was nigh, so he decided to consult with the most experienced doctors he could find to see if they had a more positive perspective on things. One of these doctors, who was by all accounts the best in the business, visited Jing and delivered *his* assessment; while it was just as pessimistic as the *wu*'s, it does seem to have been a little more medically exacting than a vague prophecy about Jing's projected gluten intake. This doctor examined Jing and told him that, sadly, he had contracted a deadly disease and that it had already reached the *gāo huāng*—the name given to the region between the heart and the diaphragm. There was nothing that could be done, said the doctor; it was just a matter of time before Jing died. While this is true of all of us in the long term, technically speaking, this thought likely offered little in the way of comfort to Jing at the time.

Jing was downhearted, the words of the *wu* ringing in his ears, convinced that death was swiftly closing in on him. However, even while plagued with worry and dread due to his supposedly impending demise, Jing nonetheless lived on as weeks turned to months! Finally, half a year after his original consultation with the *wu*, harvest time arrived and the wheat was brought in with Jing still alive and kicking. It looked as though the *wu*'s second sight might need a bit of an eye test.

Jing, who did not seem to want to be particularly gracious about the whole affair, ordered some of the harvest's wheat to be used in preparing some food for him. As his servants worked away, Jing triumphantly dragged the *wu* in to witness the result of the successful harvest, and recognise that her morbid prediction would not come true after all. Here he was, having survived to see the harvest, and as soon as this food was ready, he would prove the *wu* wrong by living to eat the new wheat, in direct contravention of what she had told him six months previously. Jing didn't seem to be in a very forgiving state of mind, either: he ordered the immediate execution of the *wu*, as punishment for her supposedly shonky prophecy, and so that was the end of her.

However, as it turns out, the prophecy was anything but shonky. Before sitting down to tuck into his freshly made food, Jing felt the need to, ah, *make some room*, so he headed to the privy. Despite surviving until the harvest, he was still a frail and feeble old man who wasn't in great condition. Consequently, when he dropped his drawers and sat down to do his business, he just . . . fell in.

The *Zuo Zhuan* is tragically short on details as to the exact circumstances of the duke's death, simply stating 'he fell in and died'. For his sake, you'd hope that he died on impact rather than drowning in a pit of foul effluvia, but however it happened, he ended up dead in the dunny—with his food sitting at the table, its wheat thoroughly uneaten. The *wu* ended up being right, all along!

When Jing's absence was noted, a servant searched for him and found his body at the bottom of the pit beneath the toilet. The servant dutifully went down to retrieve the corpse; after undertaking this immensely unpleasant task, he was rewarded with the great honour of being killed and buried with his former master. The poor servant really did have a shitty job, in more ways than one.

Ultimately, Jing's greatest legacy is joining an exclusive group of notable historical figures who suffered toilet-related deaths.[1] This probably isn't the sort of legacy most people hope for, but hey, whatever gets you into the history books.

Interestingly, Jing's death also led to the creation of a Chinese *chéngyǔ*, a four-character idiom. The doctor's prognosis—'the disease

1 We'll get to quite a few of them in due course, don't you worry.

had reached the *gāo huāng*'—became a proverb. Even today, Chinese speakers will say '*bìng rù gāo huāng*' to express the idea that something is beyond help, or past the point of saving. It's a shame they have to stick to just four characters for a *chéngyǔ*, otherwise they could have instead gone for '*gōngjué sǐ zài cèsuǒ lǐ*'—'the duke is dead in the toilet'.

2

Arrhichion of Phigalia

Died While Winning an Olympic Wrestling Bout, 564 BCE

Mixed martial arts go back a very, very long way in history. This is unsurprising, really, as one of humanity's favourite pastimes is finding clever and exciting new ways to hurt and even kill each other. Even today, in the modern age, blood sports are as popular as ever: widely publicised hand-to-hand combat events such as those put on by the UFC[1]

1 'UFC' here refers to the Ultimate Fighting Championship, famous for staging large mixed martial arts events, and not the United Fruit Company, famous for staging the overthrow of inconvenient Central American governments to sell more bananas. Despite the seemingly vast differences between these two companies, both have been in the business of leveraging violence for profit.

draw bloodthirsty audiences of millions from around the world, gathering to watch musclebound bruisers beat each other's faces in. This is a great pity. These people really should be encouraged to just sit down and *talk* about the issues they have with one another, rather than resorting to violence to solve interpersonal problems.

In any case, the history of mixed martial arts can be traced back thousands of years. In ancient Greece, it was referred to as *pankration*—a combination of boxing and wrestling, with holds and chokes and kicks thrown in along with all of the other wonderful things that martial artists do to each other's bodies. In *pankration*, which was a particularly brutal combat sport, there were only two rules: no biting and no eye-gouging—but that was only if you were fighting outside of Sparta. In Sparta, there were no rules whatsoever. You could gouge out one of your opponent's eyes and then bite the other, and the referees would just tell your opponent to stop all the whinging and get on with things.

Pankration was such a big part of ancient Greek culture that it even found its way into their myths and legends, with great heroes such as Heracles being described as expert practitioners. In Greek myth, Heracles—often referred to by his Roman name, Hercules—was one of many children born of his father Zeus's affairs, and famously had to undertake twelve labours to atone for the murder of his wife and children. Had Heracles been taken to trial for this crime, astute legal counsel would likely have advised him to plead insanity, given that he had killed his family only after having been cursed with madness by a jealous Hera, Zeus's wife.[2]

The first of Heracles' twelve labours was slaying the Nemean lion, a terrible beast with golden fur that was impervious to mortal weapons, and razor-sharp claws that could cut through any mortal armour. Heracles very neatly sidestepped these issues by engaging the lion in *pankration*, which requires the use of neither weapons nor armour, and in the end he was able to strangle the fearsome animal to death. Choosing this mode of combat was a clever move from Heracles. Assuming this bout followed the ancient customs and traditions of *pankration*, Heracles cunningly found a way to prevent the lion from biting him, as that would have been against the rules.[3]

In the somewhat more verifiable world of history, rather than in the murkier waters of myth and legend, *pankration* was an immensely popular spectator sport, exhibited at the Ancient Olympic Games from 648 BCE onwards. For the first few decades in which the games were held, from 776 to 708 BCE, the only events on the schedule were running races, so you'd imagine that the ancient Greeks welcomed a bit of variety when the pentathlon and wrestling were introduced in

---

2 Under Article 34 of the Greek Penal Code, 'a criminal act is not attributable to the perpetrator if because of a disturbance of his mental functions, or a disturbance of conscience, he did not possess the ability to acknowledge the wrongfulness of this act'. While the legal question is currently untested, one might not think it unreasonable to consider a curse of madness from a jaded, cuckolded goddess 'a disturbance of mental functions'. This is not legal advice.

3 After all, the lion was from Nemea, not Sparta.

the 18th Olympiad of 708 BCE. Boxing came along shortly thereafter, in 688 BCE, and then finally *pankration* 40 years later.

Excitingly, Olympians back then all competed completely naked. This obviously led to a lot of flopping and flapping during the running races, but also meant that *pankratists* had no clothes to grab onto while grappling with one another.[4] It also meant they had no protection from the referees, who observed bouts while armed with sticks, with which they would whack the competitors if they broke any rules. It really is a great shame that we've done away with armed referees in modern sports. Just imagine: rather than soccer referees using whistles and coloured cards while overseeing a game, they could be given paintball guns instead.

The most famous *pankratist* from the ancient Greek world was a man named Arrhichion of Phigalia. This is not only because he was never defeated in Olympic *pankration*, but also because he is the only Olympian in history to win his event . . . as a *corpse*.

Mighty Arrhichion was competing as a *pankratist* in the 54th Olympiad, in 564 BCE, having won the event at both the 52nd and 53rd Olympiads, eight and four years earlier, respectively. He was keen to come back and defend his title, and did very well throughout the tournament, eventually making it all the way to the championship bout to face off against his final opponent.

The fight began. After going back and forth, Arrhichion's opponent—whose name we sadly don't know—managed to get

4 Perhaps they found something else to grab instead.

the upper hand by forcing Arrhichion into a headlock. Positioned behind Arrhichion, he had his arm around Arrhichion's neck and his legs locked around Arrhichion's body, and then used his feet to squash Arrhichion's ghoulies. It wasn't looking good for the reigning champion, who was about to get choked out—not to mention his poor boys downstairs being crushed like overripe grapes.

But then, with a heroic, final effort—a *very* final effort, as it turned out—Arrhichion locked one of his opponent's feet in the crook of his knee, gripped it tightly and ripped it down, actually dislocating his opponent's foot from the ankle! His opponent recoiled violently in pain, immediately signalling his surrender to the referees as he did so.[5] Arrhichion had won, snatching victory from the jaws of defeat!

Well . . . sort of. Remember, Arrhichion was in a headlock when he dislocated his opponent's foot. When his opponent recoiled, he failed to release Arrhichion from the headlock first—and so *snapped Arrhichion's neck* as he pulled back in pain. This manoeuvre, tragically but altogether unsurprisingly, killed the unfortunate Arrhichion instantly.

However, as his opponent had surrendered to the referees, there was no choice other than to declare Arrhichion victorious and, therefore, the *pankration* champion of the 54th Olympiad—irrespective of his current state of animacy. You can just imagine the referees

5 Just as a modern mixed martial arts fighter might 'tap out', likely wishing they had just used their words instead of fighting.

desperately flipping through the rulebook before perhaps finally confirming, 'Ain't no rule says a dead body can't be champion!'

Arrhichion's corpse was proclaimed the winner and duly awarded the victor's customary olive-leaf wreath.[6] To this day, he remains not just history's most famous *pankratist*, but also the only Olympian—ancient or modern—to be crowned as a champion while dead. While it can be very exciting to see old Olympic records broken as athletes push themselves to new limits every four years, Arrhichion's highly unique record is probably best left uncontested.

---

6 Medals weren't awarded in the Ancient Olympic Games; victorious athletes would receive just an olive-leaf wreath and, if they were really lucky, a congratulatory slap on the arse.

3

Aeschylus

Killed by a Falling Tortoise, 456 BCE

Aeschylus is widely considered to be the father of the theatrical tragedy. Across the millennia, various forms of entertainment media have featured monumentally important and extremely popular tragedies, from Aeschylus's own trilogy *The Oresteia* and Shakespearean works such as *Hamlet* and *Macbeth*, all the way through to modern creations such as *Breaking Bad, Game of Thrones* and, of course, the pinnacle of modern cinema: the 1998 Coen brothers tragic masterpiece *The Big Lebowski.*

The way Aeschylus died, however, was anything but tragic. It was, conversely, extremely funny indeed—although probably not for Aeschylus, who wasn't really in a position to laugh about it afterwards.

Aeschylus lived an incredibly full life. Born around 525 BCE into a wealthy family who lived just north of Athens, he began writing plays in his twenties. He took a break from the world of theatre in his thirties to go and fight in the legendarily famous Battle of Marathon in 490 BCE, when Athenians and their allies came together to fight off an invading Achaemenid army led by the Persian king Darius the Great.

The Greeks won—great job, Aeschylus—and today the battle gives its name to a running race that is around 42 kilometres in length, the approximate distance between Marathon and Athens. The story goes that a courier named Pheidippides ran from Marathon to Athens to deliver news of the Greek victory, then immediately dropped dead. This is unlikely to have actually happened, however. Tales of this run began to emerge over 500 years after the Battle of Marathon, and seem to be based on a different long-distance run undertaken by Pheidippides: the ancient Greek historian Herodotus, writing only a few decades after the Battle of Marathon, tells us how Pheidippides ran not from Marathon to Athens after the battle, but from Athens to Sparta *before* the battle—a distance of over 200 kilometres—so as to request Spartan aid. If we were really going to honour Pheidippides' efforts properly, we should be commemorating his much more reliably sourced run from Athens to Sparta, but then again forcing runners to race over 200 kilometres purely for the sake of supposed historical accuracy might be too much of an ask.[1]

Aeschylus also fought in the less-famous-but-much-more-important Battles of Salamis and Plataea, helping to drive the Achaemenids out of the ancient Greek world for good, and these experiences as a soldier on the front line had a strong influence on his later work. His play *The Persians* tells the story of the Persian defeat at Salamis, and is the only surviving ancient Greek play that actually deals with events that were going on at the time it was written.

Aeschylus wrote between 70 and 90 plays, although sadly only seven of them survive today. These very important ancient works have helped to shape and develop Western literature over the centuries, in addition to being immensely popular and successful back in Aeschylus's time.

But even if only around 10 per cent of Aeschylus's plays have survived, precisely 0 per cent of Aeschylus himself has. As he lived around 2,500 years ago, perhaps this shouldn't come as much of a surprise—however, the way in which he exited this world certainly

1 Historical accuracy doesn't play much of a part in determining the length of the modern marathon, which stands at a highly scientific 42-and-a-bit kilometres, a distance that was settled upon at the 1908 London Olympic Games. Prior to this event, the marathon was run over all sorts of different distances, usually around 40 kilometres. In 1908, however, the distance was extended so the race would end in front of the Royal Box, which just so happened to be 42.195 kilometres from the starting line. This very specific distance later became the standard.

might. Before we get there, though, it's time for a brief diversion into the realm of the behaviour of a certain avian predator.

The golden eagle is one of the most widely distributed birds of prey in the northern hemisphere: it's found everywhere from Spain to Japan, from northern Canada to southern Iran. It's also found in Sicily, where it eats, among other things, tortoises.

Rather selfishly, however, tortoises don't make themselves easily edible for the golden eagle, armoured as they are with their thick shells. The golden eagle has had to find a way around this obstacle, and so has learned to pick up a tortoise in its talons, fly high up in the sky and drop the tortoise down onto rocks below. This doesn't just kill the poor thing, it also splits the shell, exposing the meat inside and allowing the eagle to enjoy a succulent chelonian meal. The golden eagle exhibits this cunning predatory behaviour today, but based on the story of Aeschylus, the species has known about this little trick for thousands of years.

In the year 456 BCE, when Aeschylus was around 69 years of age, he was visiting the Sicilian city of Gela. One day, while sitting peacefully among the rocks outside the city, he became the unwitting and probably accidental target of a lethal testudinal bombardment. A golden eagle wheeling overhead with a tortoise in its clutches perhaps mistook Aeschylus's shiny, bald head as a particularly suitable rock and dropped its quarry down from on high.

The golden eagle had murder in its heart, of course, eagerly seeking the death of the tortoise it carried as well as the meal that would come along as a consequence. Even with its murderous intentions towards the tortoise, however, this eagle probably didn't mean to also end the life of one of history's greatest playwrights—but that's what it did by dropping the tortoise. The unwitting Aeschylus was instantly struck dead by the hard shell of the tortoise, bringing the life of one of history's foremost theatrical tragedians to an end you would be more likely to expect from a theatrical comedy. If both Aeschylus and the tortoise that was killed with him were around today, and able to comment on the way they both died, they likely would express their enthusiastic agreement with the protagonist of the 1998 Coen brothers tragic masterpiece *The Big Lebowski* in saying that they, too, hate the fuckin' eagles.

4

Mithridates the Soldier

Killed by 'The Boats', 401 BCE

The story of the death of the Persian soldier Mithridates places us on a rather unsteady historical footing. It's quite a tale, full of all sorts of terrifically gory body horror, but it's probably worth noting that it may never have happened in the first place. The account of this death, written by Plutarch, a Greek historian of the first century CE, came along several centuries after it was said to have taken place.

Plutarch himself adapted his version of events from the account of another historian named Ctesias. Writing in the fifth century BCE,

Ctesias is generally considered to have subscribed to the 'never let the truth get in the way of a good story' school of narrative delivery.[1] As a result, there's reason to think that the story of poor Mithridates *might* be apocryphal. But you know what, bugger all that—it really is an incredible tale, so we're going to get into it anyway.

Back in 401 BCE, the Achaemenid Empire was ruled by King Artaxerxes II, the great-grandson of Xerxes I, the Achaemenid ruler who had been defeated at Salamis and Plataea by Aeschylus and all of his mates. Early on in his reign, Artaxerxes II faced many challenges to his throne, but he saw them all off and managed to rule for over four decades. In addition to this impressive feat, he also fathered well over a hundred kids across his reign. Given how busy he must have been with that whole business, it remains a mystery to this day how he also had the time to actually rule his empire.

In any case, one day in 401 BCE some grim tidings reached his ears: a young soldier named Mithridates had emerged, claiming to have killed Artaxerxes' brother, Cyrus the Younger, on the field of battle. As you might imagine, Artaxerxes wasn't exactly pleased by this. The emotions he went through—pain, remorse, even anger—aren't unusual on hearing about the death of a brother. However, interestingly enough, the source of these emotions wasn't some deep and abiding fraternal connection between Artaxerxes and Cyrus.

---

1 Among other things, in his writings Ctesias claimed that there was a race of people known as monopods, who had one single large foot that they could use not only to get around but also to shade themselves from the sun by lying on their backs with their foot held above them.

Artaxerxes was filled with pain, remorse, and anger not because his brother had been killed, but because *he* hadn't been the one to kill him.

As mentioned, Artaxerxes had faced challenges early in his rule. Most of these early challenges came from his brother, Cyrus the Younger, who eventually hired 10,000 Greek mercenaries to try to claim the Achaemenid throne from Artaxerxes, only to be defeated at the Battle of Cunaxa. During the battle, Artaxerxes was told, Cyrus had been killed by this young soldier Mithridates, who was now hurrying back to the Persian court to boast of his triumph to a presumably grateful Artaxerxes.

This proved to be a bad move. Rather than the adulation and acclaim he was hoping for, Mithridates was instead on the receiving end of Artaxerxes' white-hot fury. The king took being robbed of the opportunity to kill his own brother as a personal insult to his honour, and so he sentenced Mithridates to die in one of the most horrific ways you can imagine.

We turn now to Plutarch's biographical work *Life of Artaxerxes* to talk us through it.[2]

> [Artaxerxes] gave orders that Mithridates should be put to death by the torture of the boats.

2 This 1926 translation comes from the American historian Bernadotte Perrin, whose moustache is among the finest in classicist academia. Conversely, the finest Beard in classicist academia is, of course, Mary.

Okay, well, how awful could this possibly be? 'The boats' doesn't sound too bad, really. Perhaps he'll be taken by boat and marooned somewhere? Live the rest of his life on a remote island, dozing in the sun and eating coconuts? Or maybe he'll be taken on a fishing trip? Fishing trips are certainly torturously boring, so it could very well be that.

> Now, this torture of the boats is as follows. Two boats are taken, which are so made as to fit over one another closely; in one of these the victim is laid, flat upon his back; then the other is laid over the first and carefully adjusted, so that the victim's head, hands, and feet are left projecting, while the rest of his body is completely covered up.

So he's laid out like some teenage mutant ninja boatman, his extremities trapped, poking out through gaps in between two boats that have been put together like clamshells so he can't move. Not ideal.

> Then they give him food to eat, and if he refuse[s] it, they force him to take it by pricking his eyes. After he has eaten, they give him a mixture of milk and honey to drink, pouring it into his mouth, and also deluge his face with it.

Oh dear. It's probably safe to assume that he's not being forced to eat for any *good* reason, and it's starting to sound pretty torturous when they're making a great big mess of milk and honey all over his face.

> Then they keep his eyes always turned towards the sun, and a swarm of flies settles down upon his face and hides it completely. And since inside the boats he does what must needs be done when men eat and drink, worms and maggots seethe up from the corruption and rottenness of the excrement, devouring his body, and eating their way into his vitals.

'Does what needs be done when men eat and drink' is a very delicate way to put it, especially when the next sentence is all about 'the corruption and rottenness of the excrement'. Plutarch is really painting us a picture here, a fascinatingly gruesome one that kind of makes you wish your brain had a delete function.

> For when at last the man is clearly dead and the upper boat has been removed, his flesh is seen to have been consumed away, while about his entrails swarms of such animals as I have mentioned are clinging fast and eating. In this way Mithridates was slowly consumed for seventeen days, and at last died.

Oh. Okay.

Mithridates was eaten alive for *two and a half weeks* before he finally expired, for the heinous crime of killing the king's brother before the king could. In that light, perhaps the fishing trip would be preferable after all.

5

Zeuxis of Heraclea

Died of Laughter, Fourth Century BCE

Death is almost always a source of great sorrow and grief. It tears our friends and loved ones from us; it wreaks havoc and destruction on humanity in its terrible, countless forms. Death really is no laughing matter. Except, of course, when it *is*.

Quite a number of people have died of laughter. It's not a very common way to die, but it does happen. When you consider all of the awful ways a life can end, laughter might not actually be such a bad way to go. You'd be in good company, anyway: it was laughter that claimed the life of ancient Greek painter Zeuxis of Heraclea, who died sometime in the fourth century BCE.

Zeuxis was an immensely talented painter. Sadly, none of his paintings have survived the test of time, so we don't know exactly what they looked like. However, based on the descriptions of his work that have made it through to today, Zeuxis was known for his highly realistic style and his ability to use light and shadow in his work rather than just flat colour, in addition to his clever innovations when it came to composition.

He painted all sorts of stuff, from gods and historical events to nudes and still life. Zeuxis's art was greatly admired by everyone, and by all accounts he was one of the most gifted artists of his time. Although not, as was apparently proven during his lifetime, the *most* gifted, as a (likely apocryphal) story from famous Roman historian Pliny the Elder tells us. Written several centuries after Zeuxis's death, Pliny the Elder's vast work *Naturalis Historia* relates the following story not about Zeuxis's eventual death, but about one of the amusing misadventures he had while trying to prove his talent as a painter.

At some point during Zeuxis's career, he got involved in a contest with a rival painter, Parrhasius of Ephesus, to determine once and for all which one of them had the greater skill. They agreed to demonstrate their mastery of their craft by creating the most lifelike painting they possibly could before comparing the results. Both went away and worked on their paintings, then eventually reconvened to pit their works against one another.

Zeuxis was the first to unveil his painting, pulling off the cloth that covered it to reveal an exquisite image of some grapes. These grapes looked so realistic that—the story goes—*birds flew down to peck at them*. This might raise more than a few eyebrows when it comes to just how truthful this anecdote may be, but this is what Pliny had to say on the matter, and who are we to doubt him? After all, it's not as if anything else he wrote in *Naturalis Historia* might be apocryphal: stories of mythical creatures such as manticores and basilisks, tales of people who survived purely by *smelling* food rather than eating it, and instructions on how cure a toothache by injecting the stomach lining of a hare into your ear.[1]

Believe it or not, this story about the painting contest isn't even the only tale about Zeuxis that has birds wanting a taste of his realistically painted grapes. In another anecdote, Zeuxis is said to have painted a boy holding a bunch of grapes, and sure enough, birds flew down to peck at them.[2] Apparently, however, this actually disappointed Zeuxis and made him consider the painting a failure because had it *actually* been realistic from top to bottom, the birds wouldn't have come down to peck at the grapes—they would have been scared of the painted boy.

But let's get back to the contest: Zeuxis unveiled his work, the birds

---

1 All this nonsense really does appear in Pliny the Elder's *Naturalis Historia*, in addition to so much more. In fairness to him, however, Pliny did unsuccessfully try to dispel the commonly held misconception that the urine of a wild lynx would solidify and harden into a valuable gemstone called lyngurium. Research into lyngurium continued for a very long time, with one sixteenth-century text, *The Noble Lyfe and Natures of Man*, stating '*pisse baketh in ye sonne and that becommeth a ryche stone*'. No proof of lyngurium exists today, but perhaps this is due to the greed of the wretched lynx in refusing to share its treasure with us.

2 Where were these paintings displayed, that great flocks of birds were at the ready, waiting for their lunch?

came down, look at that, Zeuxis has done it again, what a hero, what a legend, how does he do it, etc. Supremely unconcerned, however, Parrhasius then asked Zeuxis to do him the honour of unveiling *his* painting, and so Zeuxis approached and reached for the cloth that covered it . . . only to find that the painting was *of the cloth itself.* Zeuxis had been utterly fooled by Parrhasius's realistic painting and, recognising he had lost, was very gracious in defeat: 'I have deceived the birds, but Parrhasius has deceived Zeuxis.'

The result of this contest didn't, thankfully, affect Zeuxis's career too much.[3] While exact details are scarce, it does seem that he remained a very sought-after artist throughout his entire career, as he continued to receive commissions from patrons across the Mediterranean, from Rome to Byzantium, painting works for the rich, the famous, and the powerful.

However, it was one of these works that brought him undone. His very last commission came from a wealthy old lady who wanted a painting of Aphrodite. As the Greek goddess of love, passion, and beauty, Aphrodite was naturally considered to be one of the most beautiful beings in existence by the ancient Greeks. She is represented in Botticelli's masterwork *The Birth of Venus*[4] and has remained a lasting symbol of feminine beauty for thousands of years.

No worries so far, then: Zeuxis just had to let rip with another of

3 Likely because, once again, it almost certainly never actually happened.

4 Venus is the Roman name for Aphrodite. The ancient Romans were far too busy to come up with their own gods, so they just plagiarised the Greek pantheon and changed all of the names so the teacher wouldn't notice.

his masterful paintings, ensuring that he suitably captured Aphrodite's divine beauty. All in a day's work for a painter of his calibre! Until, that is, his wealthy patron added in another little requirement she had for the painting: she, an elderly lady, wanted to model for it.

Zeuxis did his best to accommodate her, but more or less every representation of Aphrodite you're likely to come across depicts her as a comely youth, a glorious and immortal Olympian, immune to the ravages of time. Instead of painting Aphrodite in this fashion, though, Zeuxis was in the unenviable position of having to take a very unorthodox approach in depicting the resplendent goddess of beauty as an old woman. Nonetheless, he gave it a red-hot go, and you can only imagine how the painting began to shape up: its subject perhaps sporting an expression somewhere between divine radiance and a pained squint brought on by searching for the Werther's Originals without her glasses.

Zeuxis's masterfully realistic style eventually got the better of him. At one point, as he was painting, he burst out in laughter at what he had painted: Aphrodite as a wrinkly old lady. He found it so funny that he couldn't stop laughing, and ultimately keeled over and died, painting his own punchline that sent him to the great canvas in the sky.

Amazingly, somehow people still claim that laughter is the best medicine.

6

King Wu of Qin

Died while Lifting a Really Heavy Cauldron, 307 BCE

King Wu was just eighteen years old when he succeeded his father to the throne of the Qin state in 310 BCE, during the Warring States Period of ancient Chinese history. This period is exceptionally well named, as there were indeed a lot of states that got a fair bit of warring done during it, and Qin under King Wu was no exception.

Despite his young age—or perhaps because of it, given the general recklessness and sense of immortality that young men so often have—King Wu got stuck into these ongoing wars, having a crack at other states such as the Wei and the Han. Generally speaking, he did very well with these campaigns, although he wasn't particularly merciful to those he defeated. He reportedly beheaded up to *60,000* enemy combatants. Not personally, you'd have to assume. There are only so many hours in the day.

When he wasn't off crushing his enemies and seeing them driven before him, Wu focused on his life's passions: strength and vigour. King Wu was built like a brick shithouse, an absolute unit, all rippling muscles and throbbing veins. This bloke's chassis was like something from the cover of a men's health magazine. He was absolutely yoked, completely ripped to shreds, and had he been born a few millennia later, he likely would have made an fortune as a fitness influencer.

Instead, however, he was born to be a king, and his obsession with physical conditioning heavily influenced how he ruled. He booted out all of the stuffy career politicians who had previously filled his senior advisory positions and replaced them with muscled hunks, making it clear that brawn ruled brains in his administration. And this worked, somehow! Not only was he winning all of these battles against the Qin's hated foes, and not only was his governmental style causing the administration of the Qin state to hum along nicely, but King Wu was also strong, tall, and handsome. The complete package! Was there anything this young man couldn't do?

Well, yes, there was, apparently: powerlift a huge bronze cauldron.

Wu loved to show off his physical strength. He enjoyed wrestling and weightlifting, and he didn't waste any opportunities to demonstrate his immeasurable vigour. As much as this increased his reputation as a strong and powerful leader, it also ultimately ended his career as a strong and powerful leader.

An opportunity to exhibit his strength presented itself when another strongman, Meng Yue, challenged the king to a weightlifting contest one day. Never one to back down from a challenge such as this, King Wu took on Meng Yue, agreeing to lift a type of ceremonial bronze cauldron known as a *dǐng*. These cauldrons were a very important part of rituals and the like in ancient China, and they came in all different shapes and sizes. The one that these two men used for the contest, however, was colossal—and colossally heavy.

Once the king accepted his challenge, the beefcake Meng Yue lifted the *dǐng* with relative ease, then put it back down and looked over to his royal rival to see if King Wu would be able to equal this incredible feat of strength. Wu stepped forwards, prepared himself and then hefted the enormous cauldron off the ground. His thunderous muscles strained; his Herculean body barely kept it together as he held up the immensely heavy weight.

But then, with a sickening, splintering *crack*, the king's powerhouse rig finally failed him, as his shin bones snapped like twigs underneath the weight of the *dǐng*. Heavy lies the crown, certainly, but even heavier lies the giant bronze cauldron. This is why you never skip leg day.

Things didn't get any better for King Wu. Later that night, after his humiliating defeat in the weightlifting contest, blood started leaking from the king's eyes, which is rarely a sign that things are going well. It wasn't long after his encounter with Meng Yue that King Wu died of the injuries he had suffered while overexerting himself—he was killed not only by the weight of a gigantic bronze cauldron but also by the weight of his gigantic ego.

In the end, however, lifting this *dǐng* didn't only claim King Wu's life. The luckless Meng Yue *also* died as an indirect result of hoisting it aloft, as he was held responsible for the death of the king: he was blamed for provoking Wu into this deadly weightlifting contest. Consequently, Meng Yue was put to death for regicide—along with *the rest of his family*, just for good measure. Everyone knows that weightlifting can be a dangerous sport, but it's not often that it gets your whole family killed.

7

Pyrrhus of Epirus

Killed by a Roof Tile, 272 BCE

You may have heard of the term 'Pyrrhic victory': a triumph that costs so much to achieve it might as well have been a defeat. One of the most famous examples of a Pyrrhic victory is the poorly named Battle of Bunker Hill,[1] which took place in the opening stages of the American Revolutionary War. Technically, the British defeated the rebels and captured the Boston Peninsula, but the battle was still a disaster for them. They had far more casualties, including a huge

1 To the everlasting delight of historical pedants and 'well, actually' enthusiasts everywhere, the Battle of Bunker Hill didn't take place on Bunker Hill: it was instead fought on nearby Breed's Hill.

number of officers, and learned the sharp lesson that these upstart colonists weren't to be underestimated.

Why do we call victories like these 'Pyrrhic'? To answer that, we have to go back more than 2,000 years, to an ancient Greek king called Pyrrhus of Epirus. Pyrrhus spent much of his monarchical career fighting more or less anyone and anything, and while he won plenty of battles, some of these victories came at an *extremely* steep cost.

Pyrrhus took the throne of Epirus in 307 BCE, when he was just a young boy. Unfortunately for him, he was ousted as king before long, replaced by a usurper named Neoptolemus II in 302 BCE. However, in what proved to be a very good move for his career, Pyrrhus married the stepdaughter of the powerful Ptolemy I Soter, the first ruler of Ptolemaic Egypt, and Ptolemy I was generous enough to restore Pyrrhus to his throne as co-king with Neoptolemus II, whom Pyrrhus promptly had assassinated. Sometimes the simplest solution is the best.

Back in charge of his kingdom in his own right, Pyrrhus went from strength to strength. He established Epirus as a formidable regional power, winning many traditional, non-Pyrrhic victories against other Greek kingdoms that stood against him. But then, in 282 BCE, he went to war with the Roman Republic, and this is when the Pyrrhic victories started to come in thick and fast.

Pyrrhus accepted an invitation from Tarentum, a Greek city on the Italian peninsula, to help defend them from the Romans. Pyrrhus was happy to have some new people to fight, as he'd more or less run out of targets in the Greek world, and so he loaded tens of thousands of troops onto a fleet of ships and sailed them over to Tarentum, kicking off the Pyrrhic War.

The two major battles of the Pyrrhic War were the Battle of Heraclea and the Battle of Asculum, and these battles ended up becoming very famous indeed. Pyrrhus was heavily outnumbered in the Battle of Heraclea, which saw 35,000 men under his command face off against a much larger Roman army of 45,000. However, Pyrrhus demonstrated his tactical brilliance to overcome the larger Roman force, although in doing so his army took enormous losses.

Similarly, during the Battle of Asculum, Pyrrhus was able to carry the day against the Romans; however, despite emerging victorious, his forces were almost completely wiped out. Pyrrhus was there, getting stuck in himself, fighting shoulder to shoulder with his men, leading them on to victory—but this triumph came at an immense cost.

The Romans could replenish their dead and wounded with fresh troops thanks to their home-ground advantage and proximity to Rome, whereas the Greek losses were felt more keenly as soldiers couldn't be so easily replaced from across the Ionian Sea. This led to a famous quote after the Battle of Asculum: according to the ancient Greek historian Plutarch,[2] Pyrrhus was supposed to have said, 'If we are victorious in one more battle with the Romans, we shall be utterly ruined.'

---

2 The same ancient Greek historian who was good enough to let us know about Mithridates being sentenced to 'the boats'.

It wasn't long after these two victories, therefore, that Pyrrhus threw in the towel and withdrew from the Italian peninsula without having made any real gains, despite winning 100 per cent of the battles he fought there. It was this disastrous string of victories that gave rise to the term 'Pyrrhic victory'.

You might think that this isn't the sort of thing you'd want as your historical legacy; it's a real piece of bad luck for Pyrrhus, remembered for being so bad at winning that he had to retreat after doing it! All things considered, though, he would probably be glad to find out he's remembered for *that*, rather than being remembered for how he died.

Pyrrhus continued to fight more wars after his ill-fated campaign against the Romans. He fought Carthaginians in Sicily for a while, then eventually returned to the other side of the Ionian Sea and got back to his core competency of fighting other Greeks. It was in one such fight he finally met his end, during an invasion of the Peloponnesian Peninsula in 272 BCE.

Pyrrhus laid siege to Sparta, then marched on to the nearby city of Argos, breaching its walls. As already established, Pyrrhus liked to be in the thick of things, fighting alongside the soldiers he commanded—however, this time, he wouldn't emerge from the battlefield alive. During the hand-to-hand fighting on the streets of Argos, Pyrrhus was wounded by a man with a spear. He rounded on his attacker, intent upon avenging the blow, not knowing that the time of his death was finally upon him.

At this point you might be thinking, alright, an ancient Greek king being killed by a spearman during a street battle—there's nothing particularly strange about that. How did this guy manage to make it into this book?

Well, it wasn't the spearman who killed Pyrrhus. Rather, it was the *mother* of the spearman, who, seeing the danger her son was in from this furious Epirote king, chucked a roof tile at him. Her aim was true, the roof tile came down on Pyrrhus's head, and Pyrrhus collapsed to the ground. The blow from the tile itself may have killed him immediately, but if it didn't, the subsequent decapitation that took place while he lay there prone certainly did.

So, overall, Pyrrhus should be glad that the term bearing his name is 'Pyrrhic victory' and not 'Pyrrhic *defeat*'—which could be used to describe being killed by an angry mum with a knack for improvised weaponry.

8

Chrysippus of Soli

Also Died of Laughter, 206 BCE

The painter Zeuxis isn't the only notable ancient Greek figure to have died from laughter. It's probably fair to argue that he isn't even the most famous: you may have heard of Chrysippus of Soli, who died of laughter after seeing, of all things, a donkey eating figs. Yeah. Some ancient Greeks must have had a very strange concept of comedy.

Chrysippus was born in 279 BCE, in the ancient city of Soli. He moved to Athens to pursue his philosophical studies, attending the Platonic Academy under the tutelage of second-string ancient Greek philosophers that no one has really heard of, such as Lacydes of Cyrene and Arcesilaus the Sceptic. This was over a century after huge headliners such as Plato and Socrates had died, and even if a heavy hitter such as Diogenes of Sinope had still been around, good luck getting him out of his wine jar and down to the Platonic Academy to teach all the young students.[1]

During his studies, it very quickly emerged that Chrysippus had a sharp intellect and was a voracious learner. He was a prolific writer (although sadly not much of his writing has survived to the present day), and quickly rose in reputation and esteem among other philosophers of the time.

While Chrysippus wrote extensively on all sorts of topics—mathematics, physics, ethics, fate—his principal work was on Stoicism, specifically Stoic logic. As philosophically robust as Chrysippus was, reading his work is as dull as watching grass dry, filled with conditional propositions and indemonstrable syllogisms and other nonsense that philosophers demand everyone else take seriously.

Perhaps his lifelong dedication to some of the most boring stuff you'll ever come across played a part in his death. Before witnessing a donkey eating figs, perhaps the most amusing thing Chrysippus had ever seen was an incorrectly constructed disjunctive syllogism that failed to properly establish the requisite exclusivity between its constituent propositions, thereby undermining the overall validity of its deductive structure. No wonder he died of laughter: if most of

1 For more amusing details on Diogenes of Sinope and the wine jar in which he lived, why not have a listen to episode 89 of the tinpot history podcast *Half-Arsed History*?

his work is anything to go by, it might have been the first time he'd ever done it.[2]

Anyway, Chrysippus did very well for himself as a philosopher even in his own time, rising to become the head of the Stoic school of the Platonic Academy in 230 BCE, at the age of 49. Death finally came for him at the age of 73. According to the historian and biographer Diogenes Laërtius, the story goes that one day Chrysippus spotted the aforementioned donkey eating the aforementioned figs, and found it absolutely hilarious. As the donkey finished munching away, Chrysippus, bent double with laughter, called out to his servant to give the donkey some wine to wash down the figs. Then, finding this joke about the wine equally funny, he continued to laugh uncontrollably until he keeled over, dead.

In the end, not only did Chrysippus die of laughter, but he also died laughing *at his own joke*, which was . . . suggesting that a fig-eating donkey be given wine. Sounds like you had to be there.

2 Honestly, if you ever find yourself in danger of dying of laughter, just open up a bit of Chrysippus's work and have a quick read. It's just about the least funny thing ever written; the average shopping list has more humour in it.

9

Agrippina the Younger

Killed by . . . Actually, We're Honestly Not Quite Sure, 59 CE

Few women were as important and influential in the early history of the Roman Empire than Agrippina the Younger, who is remembered as a cunning and ambitious figure who stopped at nothing in her pursuit of power. Through clever political manoeuvres, ruthless plots, and the orchestration of quite a few assassinations, Agrippina would in time rise to become a Roman empress. However, when you live by the sword, you die by the sword, and after a lifetime of murderous scheming, Agrippina would herself become the victim of a murderous scheme. Almost two millennia later, we're just not sure exactly what *kind* of scheme.

Born in 15 CE, Agrippina was a scion of the famous Julio-Claudian dynasty, and she was related to all five of the dynasty's emperors. Not only was she the sister of the emperor Caligula, but she was also the great-granddaughter of the mighty emperor Augustus, the great-niece of the emperor Tiberius and the niece of the emperor Claudius. Evidently deciding that her familial connection with her uncle wasn't close enough, she would eventually go on to take Claudius as her third husband—and as she did, he became a stepfather to her son, Nero, the last of the Julio-Claudian emperors.

Marriage was just one of the many tools Agrippina used to advance her political career in imperial Rome—she was known for her constant scheming and a readiness to do more or less anything to get ahead. And get ahead she certainly did: at the apex of her career, she was one of the most powerful people in the Roman Empire.

As we all know, however, with great power comes a great number of determined and dedicated enemies with an impressive array of sharp implements, and it seems that, in the end, Agrippina's ruthless ambition led to her downfall. Her death is one of the most infamous to have occurred throughout the treacherous political history of the early Roman Empire.

Agrippina was thrust into the world of imperial scheming at a young age, when her father, the famous general Germanicus, was poisoned—likely on the orders of the emperor Tiberius, her great-uncle.

Agrippina was forced into exile as her mother, Agrippina the Elder, sought vengeance on Tiberius until it sent her to an early grave.

Finding her feet, however, Agrippina the Younger made a clever political marriage to her very well connected cousin,[1] Gnaeus Domitius Ahenobarbus. His wealth and influence helped her make a proper entrance into the world of imperial Roman politics. When her brother Caligula became emperor in 37 CE, her position improved further—until, that is, she was implicated in a plot to assassinate Caligula, leading to another period of exile.

Agrippina wasn't the only one in Rome who wanted Caligula dead,[2] and in 41 CE an assassination plot against the emperor was successfully carried out, thereby emptying the imperial throne. It was another relative of Agrippina's who would fill it: her uncle, Claudius, who brought Agrippina back from exile. She didn't waste any time in her continued climb up the political ranks, swiftly marrying the wealthy consul Gaius Sallustius Passienus Crispus in the wake of her first husband's death. Unusually for Agrippina, based on her other marriages, her second husband doesn't seem to have been a blood relation. In any case, it's thought that Agrippina promptly orchestrated Passienus's

---

1 Ancient Romans really didn't seem to see the harm in marrying their cousins. Consequently, the Julio-Claudian dynasty's family tree looks like a bowl of spaghetti.

2 This is unsurprising. Some of the reported highlights from Caligula's short time as emperor included him proclaiming himself as a god to the people of Rome, murdering much of his family, shagging the wives of leading senators, declaring war on the sea, and making plans to name his favourite horse, Incitatus, as consul (although this never actually came about, in the end).

death. While many historians will assure you that she did this to inherit his money, don't discount the possibility that she wanted to get back on the market so she could return to her passion for marrying close family members. Indeed, her next marriage was to the emperor Claudius himself, who just so happened to be her uncle—this marriage was deeply scandalous, even back then, and special legal exceptions had to be granted for it to go ahead. Ultimately, however, in 49 CE, Agrippina ended up as the empress of Rome, and even managed to convince Claudius to adopt her son, Nero, as his heir.

Claudius died in 54 CE, after being poisoned, and Nero quickly ascended to the imperial throne, at just sixteen years of age. Given these two pieces of information, you might have thought that Agrippina was in some way involved in Claudius's untimely and highly suspicious death—and you would be correct. She almost certainly was.

Now, as mother of the young emperor, Agrippina was able to rule through him. Her domineering ambition sidelined the teenage Nero, whose querulous protests were useless in the face of his mother's iron will. Poor young Nero—with his pimples and peach fuzz and half-broken voice—was a political pawn of the increasingly powerful Agrippina.

Agrippina sat in pride of place at the Roman imperial court. She attended meetings of the senate (although from behind a curtain, lest the debating senators lose their minds at the sight of a *woman* in politics), and she had her likeness minted onto coins alongside that of her son. She was a shrewd and calculating woman, who wielded her authority like a knife. And she wasn't the only one wielding something like a knife: the assassins in her employ also wielded, well, their *knives* in a similar fashion.

Agrippina kept an unyielding grip on power through the assassination of any and all political opponents who might stand in her way, and also a few people whom she just didn't like. She had other potential claimants to the imperial throne murdered, she did away with up-and-coming rivals who might undermine her position, and she drove one particularly unfortunate bloke to suicide because she liked the look of his gardens and wanted them for herself.[3]

But Agrippina's time at the top of the political heap wasn't to last. As Nero grew older, he steadily diminished his mother's influence over him, the political power she held, and her status at the imperial court. This wasn't good for Rome; the best years of Nero's time as emperor are generally considered to be those when Agrippina was the de facto ruler. Once Nero completely threw off her hold on him, it only got worse from there, and to this day Nero is remembered as one of the worst emperors in Roman history.[4]

---

3 This man's name was Titus Statilius Taurus, and he had poured his significant wealth into the creation of the beautiful Taurian Gardens in central Rome. Agrippina stirred up charges of sorcery against him, causing him to take his own life—after which she confiscated the gardens on behalf of the imperial government.

4 However, contrary to common belief, Nero didn't 'fiddle while Rome burned'. Nero was indeed a talented musician, and Rome did indeed suffer a terrible fire during his reign in 64 CE, but Nero didn't and *couldn't have* fiddled while the city burned, for the simple reason that fiddles hadn't yet been invented. Nor did he play the lyre, his preferred instrument, while the city went up in flames—indeed, some sources indicate that he actually went out and helped with the relief efforts. Even so, he was still a pretty shit emperor.

Merely removing himself from under his mother's political thrall wasn't enough for Nero, however, who still considered Agrippina a threat to his reign, even after he had stripped her of her titles and prestige. He resolved to deal with this situation once and for all by arranging for her to be killed. The apple didn't fall far from the tree, it seems.

But here is where we get to the rather interesting final chapter in Agrippina the Younger's life: we know that she died on Nero's orders, but we don't know exactly *how* she died. This is due to there being three different accounts from three different ancient Roman historians—Cassius Dio, Suetonius, and Tacitus—which are not only highly contradictory but also very likely embellished and exaggerated, as all of these historians were pretty unashamed in their efforts to paint Nero in as bad a light as possible. We may never know the exact truth behind the death of Agrippina, but here, at least, are the accounts given by these three historians. You're free to pick your favourite.

Cassius Dio asserts that Nero had a specially designed ship built, and organised for his mother to be taken aboard it. This ship had a bottom that could open up while out at sea, apparently causing Agrippina to fall into the water below, where she was expected to drown. She did not, however, and instead managed to swim back to shore—so Nero took a rather more direct route and had an assassin stab her to death,[5] before publicly denouncing his mother as a traitor

---

5 Perhaps this assassin, as part of killing Agrippina in the most simple and straightforward way possible, stabbed her with Occam's razor.

with murderous designs on him (not altogether implausible, in fairness).

Suetonius tells us that Nero first tried using poison to do away with Agrippina, an effort that demonstrated he really was his mother's son. Agrippina, however, reportedly had an antidote on hand for all three of the attempts that Nero made with poison, and so Nero took a different approach: one that was so *very* different that it could best be described as—not to put too fine a point on it—completely made up by Suetonius. Nero apparently had a device constructed that would *drop ceiling tiles on her while she was in bed*. This, shockingly, wasn't successful in killing Agrippina. Suetonius then tells a similar story to the one laid out by Cassius Dio. Nero had Agrippina taken out on a ship before staging a collision with another vessel so she would take to a small, leaky boat to escape the damage. The boat didn't sink as intended, Agrippina survived, and so it was back to the direct method instead: Nero ordered her assassination and denounced her as a traitor once she was dead.

Finally, the account written by Tacitus contains elements from both of the stories we've just covered. After failing with more conventional plots and schemes involving stabbings and poisonings and all of the other things with which Agrippina had been expertly involved for years, Nero ordered the construction of a deliberately leaky and unsound boat that was sure to sink, and he had his mother taken out on it. On this boat, however, the ceiling collapsed—kind of like Suetonius's ludicrous ceiling-tile machine—almost crushing her to death. The boat then began to sink, Agrippina escaped to shore, and, most implausibly of all, she failed to realise that the whole thing had been an assassination attempt. Nero then abandoned all pretence and just sent soldiers to kill her; they barged into her villa and stabbed her to death in her bed.

With all of these accounts laid out, what can we conclude from them about the actual fate of Agrippina? Honestly, very little. There are common elements that weave their way through these accounts—boats being sunk deliberately, dangerously unstable ceilings and a *lot* of stabbing—but the fact of the matter is that we just don't know exactly how Agrippina died.

After a life of murderous plots and deadly schemes,[6] she would fall victim to one herself, perpetrated by her own son—albeit a pretty ham-fisted and poorly executed one. Perhaps the apple *did* fall some distance from the tree, after all.

---

6 An upper estimate of Agrippina's body count totals about a dozen victims.

10

Saint Lawrence

Roasted Alive, 258 CE

Christian saints are given all sorts of weird portfolios. For instance, there's Saint Drogo, who is venerated as the patron saint of shepherds, cafe owners, and ugly people. What are Catholics trying to say about shepherds and cafe owners? Alternatively, there's Saint Fiacre, whose very diverse portfolio of patronages includes gardeners, taxi drivers and *people with haemorrhoids*. So the next time you're out in the garden and your 'roids are giving you trouble, offer up a quick prayer to Saint Fiacre—maybe he'll call you a cab to the chemist so you can grab some Preparation H.

Of all the Christian saints, however, the one with the most

amusingly appropriate patronages is Saint Lawrence, who is the patron saint of both comedians and chefs. Why? Because of the manner of his death.

Lawrence was born in 225 CE in the Roman imperial province of Hispania Tarraconensis, in what is today Spain. As an adult, while visiting the city of Caesaraugusta,[1] he met the man who would go on to become Pope Sixtus II. Sixtus took Lawrence back to Rome with him, and when he became pope in 257 CE, he ordained Lawrence as one of his deacons and put him in charge of alms for the poor.

Lawrence did very well for himself under Sixtus, rising to the position of archdeacon of Rome. It wasn't to last, though. The very next year, 258 CE, the Roman emperor Valerian officially ordered the persecution of Christians.

Christianity was, of course, a very young religion at this stage. Valerian wasn't mucking about in trying to stamp it out, either: he came for the Christians very hard indeed, decreeing that all bishops, deacons, and priests be put to death. On top of that, any wealth or goods they had would be confiscated by the imperial treasury.

Rather obviously, one of the first Christians to meet an untimely end was Pope Sixtus II. The most high-profile Christian of the time, he was arrested within a few days of the imperial edict and executed more or less straight away. Lawrence was devastated, as you might expect, because he'd lost a man who was not just his mentor but also

1 Today the city is known as Zaragoza—its modern name is a corruption of Caesaraugusta. This is a purely informative note; there's no cheap gag here this time, sorry.

his good friend. To make things worse, he knew it wouldn't be long before the Romans came for him as well, in his position as archdeacon of Rome.

He was right about this: shortly after the death of Sixtus, the imperial treasury came a-knocking, with the prefect of Rome demanding that Lawrence—who, you'll remember, was responsible for a sizeable proportion of the wealth of the Church in his role as an almoner to the poor—hand over the Church's cash. Rather than give all this money to Emperor Valerian and the Roman authorities, Lawrence put the call out and had as many of the city's poor as possible turn up and take it off his hands instead. He gave away almost every last scrap of wealth the Church had to impoverished citizens of Rome, and then, when the authorities officially summoned him to hand over the treasures of the Church, he decided to completely take the piss.

Instead of carting along gold and jewels and other items of immense value, Lawrence turned up at the imperial treasury with a bunch of the city's poor, people who were old, blind, or disabled, and presented them to the prefect, telling him that *this* was the true treasure of the Church. Touché.

Lawrence knew what he was doing, he knew what was coming for him, and so it seems that he was determined to have a laugh at the Romans' expense before they executed him. Predictably, the prefect was furious with Lawrence for this little stunt, and so condemned him to death then and there. However, the prefect decided that Lawrence wasn't going to get off easy with a quick execution, oh no.

Instead, Lawrence was in for a slow and painful death: the prefect ordered that Lawrence be tied to a big grill and roasted slowly over a fire.[2] Lawrence accepted his fate and went along to his execution willingly enough. Understandable, really; there are certainly upsides to being roasted alive. Not only will it leave you with a glowing tan, but it's also a great way to sweat off those extra pounds.

Lawrence was tied up and popped on the grill like a rotisserie chicken. But we know that this bloke liked to take the piss—while being roasted alive, Lawrence called out to the watching Romans: 'Turn me over, I'm well done on this side!'

And so it was that, after he died, Saint Lawrence became the patron saint of—very appropriately—not just comedians, but chefs as well.

2 Some accounts contest the idea that Lawrence was roasted alive, instead claiming he was beheaded. While many historians believe beheading to be a more likely fate for Lawrence, this particular chapter will take the Ridley Scott Approach to Historical Accuracy in Entertainment Media and won't let the truth get in the way of a good story.

11

Emperor Valerian

Taxidermised with Molten Gold, 260 CE

Valerian—the Roman emperor whose dedication to the persecution of Christians led to the death of Saint Lawrence—ended up suffering a pretty strange and very gruesome death himself.

Born around 199 CE, Valerian led the life of the career politician. He held offices such as consul and *princeps senatus*—leader of the senate—before eventually being proclaimed as emperor in 253 after the death of Emperor Aemilianus, who ruled for just three months.

This was during a time in Roman history when they were going through emperors like Australia was going through prime ministers in the 2010s. Between 235 CE and 284 CE, there were approximately

25 different emperors—an average of around one every two years[1]—so it's no wonder that this period is known as the Crisis of the Third Century. And, to be quite honest, Valerian's reign didn't ease the ongoing crisis all that much. He spent his time as emperor not only going after the Christians but also desperately attempting to suppress various rebellions, coping with public health crises brought on by the plague, and fighting off opportunistic invaders that were making moves on Rome while it was weakened.

Of all the enemies Valerian went up against, the Persians were the most significant. Why? Because, in the year 260 CE, Valerian became the first Roman emperor in history to be taken prisoner, when he was captured alive by the Persians during the Battle of Edessa. Valerian's capture was a disaster for Rome and resulted in his son and co-emperor, Gallienus, becoming emperor in his own right. Gallienus then had to deal with the enormous political tribulations that came with the capture of a Roman emperor; but he didn't have it half as bad as the ill-fated Valerian, who had to deal with the enormous *personal* tribulations that came with being a Roman emperor who had been captured.

Valerian was treated *abysmally* by his Persian captors during his all-expenses-paid holiday to the exotic lands to the east. His luxurious stay in a Persian prison resort included indulging in daily beatings carefully administered by seasoned specialists, enjoying a tantalising

1 Between 2010 and 2020, Australia had five different people serve as prime minister, so the simile in the previous sentence is actually more valid than you might have thought.

selection of non-existent delicacies as he experienced the transformative power of starvation, and escaping to a world of unparalleled relaxation as the Persian emperor himself, Shapur I, gave Valerian sumptuous back massages with his feet while using him as a footstool to mount his horse.

It's unclear exactly how long Valerian survived as a prisoner. It could have been years, or months, or perhaps only weeks. In any case, however long he stuck around in the Imperial Persian Serenity Spa and Detention Centre, it was an absolutely miserable experience for the poor bastard.

In time, Valerian could bear this ongoing humiliation no longer. After having an absolute gutful of this treatment, he offered Shapur a huge ransom for his release back to the Romans. Apparently, Shapur carefully considered Valerian's offer of the bestowment of great wealth for his safe return to Rome, and duly responded by bestowing great wealth on Valerian instead: he strung up Valerian and gave him the once-in-a-lifetime experience of having molten gold poured down his throat.[2] How's that for a ransom?

Needless to say, this killed Valerian on the spot.[3] But it gets worse! After his death, Valerian's corpse was skinned and then stuffed, and displayed as a *trophy* by Shapur, who seems to have been in need of

2 None of this is particularly well verified; this is just what we're told by the work of Roman historians such as Lactantius, who was weirdly anti-Persian and may have made Shapur out to be much worse than he actually was.

3 Just in case there was any lingering doubt about the potential lethality of a bellyful of molten gold.

an *actual* spa retreat, as skinning and stuffing a Roman emperor are hardly the sorts of things you do in a tranquil and relaxed state of mind.

In any case, it was a nasty way for Valerian to go, you'll agree. Perhaps he should have just stuck with being used as a mounting block.

12

Emperor Valentinian I

Got So Pissed Off He Just Died, 375 CE

The Roman emperor Valentinian I is sometimes known to history as Valentinian the Great due to his successes in fighting the enemies of the Roman Empire. He campaigned against Germanic tribes to the north and nomads to the east, strengthened and fortified the empire's borders, overcame rebellions and conspiracies, and established his own dynasty of subsequent emperors, so it's fair to say he might be deserving of his title as Valentinian the Great. However, based on how he died, perhaps he should be known to history as Valentinian Who Needs to Chill Out Just a Little Bit There Mate, Come On Now.

Born in 321 CE, Valentinian served as an army officer early on in life, joining the Roman legions in his late teenage years. He didn't fare too well as an officer, though, ultimately suffering a disastrous and embarrassing defeat at the hands of the Germanic Alamanni tribe that saw him stripped of his command and sent into political exile.

His career recovered remarkably in the coming years, however. He turned things around to the point that when the imperial throne was empty in 364 CE, and after a few other candidates had declined to become emperor, it was Valentinian who was eventually offered the position. He accepted it readily, and as a seasoned campaigner with decades of experience in the military, he very characteristically spent much of his time as emperor fighting wars all over the place. As the old saying goes, 'Find a job you love, and you'll never have to work a day in your life.'[1]

Valentinian campaigned in Gaul, the British Isles, and along the Rhine, he went after Germanic tribes such as the Alamanni—he had a score to settle there—and consolidated his rule by putting down the various revolts that emerged against him. Generally speaking, he was a pretty effective emperor; Rome had certainly seen worse, in any case. When you've had emperors who became famous for announcing that they wanted to name a horse as a consul, the bar is set pretty low.[2]

---

1 This is an 'old saying' that has been, at various points, attributed to everyone from Confucius to Mark Twain. As writer Tim Duggan once put it, 'No one actually knows who said it first, but whoever it was, they were lying.'

2 It was Caligula who did that, for readers who may have skipped that particular note in the chapter about Agrippina. If you skipped that note, though, what made you decide to read this one?

Even if Valentinian was one of the better Roman emperors, he was still a real bastard of a bloke; in particular, he was famous for his temper, which he lost more often than a sock in a dryer. Valentinian would blow a gasket at the slightest provocation, like a dad trying to tie down a trailer before a camping trip, and the people who worked both with and for him were terrified of getting in his bad books. This was because, in addition to being filled with rage, Valentinian also took unfortunate pleasure in being needlessly cruel—especially to his servants and attendants. Servants who displeased him ran the risk of being executed on a whim, and not in a particularly pleasant manner, either. Valentinian kept two pet bears, named Golden Crumb and Innocence, and he had a bad habit of very enthusiastically feeding people to them.

Clearly, Valentinian really was a rather cranky old bastard. As much as he loved military campaigning, he seemed to love blowing his top even more, and unfortunately for him it was this that would kill him in the end. In 375 CE, his temper got the better of him in a very final sense.

That year, Valentinian was off giving the business to various Germanic tribes, going after the Quadi, in particular, who lived along the Danube. The Romans went about looting, pillaging, and razing; the Quadi were tasting Valentinian's red-hot wrath, and it seemed that they didn't have the palate for it. So, eventually, the Quadi sued for peace, sending envoys to Valentinian to try to bring an end to his depredations—and they certainly succeeded in doing so, although perhaps not in the way they anticipated.

Valentinian offered a stringent and unforgiving peace settlement, which the Quadi were more or less forced to accept because their other alternative was continuing to have their teeth kicked in by the Romans. Nonetheless, the envoys told Valentinian precisely what they thought of the whole situation, and, needless to say, they weren't overwhelmingly complimentary. For all of his talents as emperor, Valentinian never became particularly adept at accepting constructive criticism, and as a result of these Quadi envoys speaking their minds like this, he flew right off the handle. He started bellowing at these upstart messengers, giving them the tongue-lashing of their lives: how *dare* they speak to him, the Roman emperor, in this way!

Valentinian continued to blow shit through these beleaguered Quadi envoys, getting more and more heated as he did so. This wasn't a sensible way for him to deal with the big feelings he was having: research today indicates that this sort of extreme anger and the emotional outbursts it triggers may be linked to a heightened possibility of stroke. It's very likely Valentinian didn't know this, given that he lived at a time when contemporary medical beliefs prescribed drinking the blood of a fallen gladiator for epilepsy.[3] In any case, even if Valentinian suspected that losing his temper might be detrimental to his health, it did absolutely nothing to make him try to calm down: his fury knew no bounds.

3 This is a theory that hasn't been tested these days with all that much scientific rigour; excusable, given the general lack of gladiators in the modern world. If only they hadn't cancelled the TV show, research could have continued.

It's believed that during anger-fuelled outbursts like this, the hormones that your body releases increase your heart rate and blood pressure, while simultaneously restricting the dilation of blood vessels—and this seems to have happened to Valentinian, because halfway through his raging tirade against the envoys, he suffered a massive cerebral haemorrhage, keeled over, and died.

Maybe we should give the Quadi some credit. It could be that they were centuries ahead of their time when it came to the medical understanding of the dangers of strokes, and this, coupled with their knowledge of Valentinian's furious temper, saw them pull off one of the most cunning assassinations in history. Whatever the case, it doesn't seem that Valentinian's death ruffled too many feathers. Certainly those close to him wouldn't have complained—they no longer had to worry about being fed to a pet bear named Innocence.

After a lifetime of violence and anger, it was probably no surprise that Valentinian was brought low by his own uncontrollable temper. The emperor left behind a cautionary tale about the dangers of unchecked anger, as well as the life-saving potential of a few deep breaths.

13

King Louis III and King Charles VIII of France

Killed by Smacking Their Heads on (Different) Doorways, 882 and 1498

Kings die of all sorts of things. Plots and schemes, personally leading armies into war, or—if they really stuff things up—being at the wrong end of a headsman's axe. It's not often that a king dies after bumping his head on a doorway, but it has happened.

Twice.

And both kings were French.

Statistically speaking, given that there were exactly 50 different kings of France,[1] this means that the job came with a 4 per cent chance of dying after bonking your head on a lintel.[2]

King Louis III of France was born in the 860s, and in 879 he came to rule the Kingdom of West Francia, the precursor state to France itself. Louis wasn't even twenty, but he didn't muck about as a fresh-faced, eager young king: he immediately got into gear and went about kicking arses up and down his kingdom in the spirit of the grand military traditions of the French.

People love to get after the French as so-called 'cheese-eating surrender monkeys', but despite what these worn-out clichés tell us, history has proven that the French are actually *very* good at war. Since the time of King Charles the Bald in 843, the French have won 159 wars and lost just 51, while 25 ended either inconclusively or in a draw. That's a 68 per cent win rate across over a thousand years of history![3] The next time you feel like poking fun at the French for their lack of prowess in war, just remember there's a

---

1 This number starts with Charles the Bald in 843, and includes the three kings and two emperors that ruled France after the French Revolution.

2 While you can make the argument that an emperor isn't a king and therefore shouldn't be included in the calculation, reducing the number of total French kings to 48 doesn't result in a statistically significant difference in the probability of doorway-related royal deaths, increasing it by just 0.167 per cent.

3 On top of this, people who so eagerly mock the French for their performance in the two World Wars seem to forget that the French were actually on the winning side for *both* of those wars.

better-than-two-thirds chance they'll hand you your *derrière* on a *plateau d'argent*.

Anyway, in what was—as has now been firmly established—the *actual* tradition of French military history, young King Louis III beat the marauding Vikings in the north, he fought his cousin Charles the Fat to the south-east, he expanded his power and territory enormously, and then, beloved by his people for all of his triumphs at such a very young age, he whacked his head on a doorframe and died.

Some stories tell us that a horse was involved: Louis leaped astride a horse, which then charged through a doorway, and the unfortunate young king clocked his head on the way through. Other sources say it was just a regular doorway that he somehow managed to brain himself on as he went through in a great hurry. Whatever the case, everyone seems to be in agreement as to the reason that he was going through this particular doorway at such a recklessly lethal speed: he was pursuing one of the ageless pastimes of the teenage boy; namely, chasing a girl. Apparently, this girl ran through the front doorway to her house as Louis chased her, and when he went to follow her inside—either on horseback or on foot—he smacked his head so hard that it killed him on the spot.

This certainly adds up. After all, teenage boys don't tend to exercise the best judgement when chasing girls.[4] It's fair to say that teenage boys aren't generally known for using their heads; except in this case, Louis *did* use his head . . . in an altogether very final way.

---

4 Or at all, really.

But, believe it or not, there's another French king who died after his forehead had an unexpected *rendez-vous* with a doorframe: King Charles VIII. Known to history by the very agreeable epithet Charles the Affable, Charles VIII is lucky to have dodged the somewhat more appropriate Charles the Spatially Unaware.

He was born in 1470 and took the French throne in 1483, at the tender age of thirteen; another teenage French king, another lethal doorframe. His reign is remembered for ongoing strife with mutinous barons, a marriage of uncertain validity to a Breton duchess, and his conquest of the Italian peninsula, thanks to the might of French gunpowder artillery.[5] However, his reign was cut short—as short as Charles probably wishes he had been when hurrying through the doorway that killed him.

Listen: Charles was a busy man. He was the king of France. He had a million things to do. He had to oversee his realm, manage its debts, keep his subjects happy, rule with grace and composure, keep those bastard barons in line, and who knows what else. He was *always* in a hurry, but on 7 April 1498, he was in a *particular* hurry.

Why? No, he wasn't chasing a girl—he was late in arriving to watch a game of tennis. It seems that Charles the Affable wasn't *quite* as affable as his distant predecessor.

As Charles rushed through the castle to where the game was to be held, he ran through the section where the men who lived and worked at the castle would go to have a cheeky slash. So not only

5 Would you look at that: it's another win for the French. *Quelle surprise!*

did it stink of piss, but the ground was also wet and slippery—and Charles raced right through it. There was no bright yellow '*Attention: Plancher Mouillé*' sign to be seen; it was an occupational health and safety nightmare. Charles slipped like someone in an ad for a shonky personal injury attorney and smashed his head against a doorframe.

In a daze, he got up and continued on to watch the game of tennis he was hurrying to attend, but shortly thereafter he collapsed and fell into a coma: one from which he would never awake. Charles died a few hours later, and he went down in history as the second—the *second*—French king to die after bonking his head.

Years later, the Palace of Versailles became the preferred royal residence for French kings, from the time of Louis XIV onwards. If you ever visit this immensely famous palace and wander through its opulent rooms and halls, take a moment to notice how tall the doorways are. Coincidence? Surely not. Clearly, French royals learned their lesson from Louis III and Charles VIII when making Versailles their new home, and weren't taking any more chances when it came to the potential lethality of lintels. This must also be why you don't see any pictures of French kings on stilts.

14

Emperor Basil I

Dragged Through a Forest by a Murderous Deer, 886

Basil I was a Byzantine emperor who died in very interesting circumstances in 886. Unlike most Byzantine emperors who suffered untimely deaths, Basil wasn't assassinated—unless the deer that killed him had a secret political agenda.

The realm we refer to as the Byzantine Empire was one of the successor states of the Roman Empire, after its split in the late fourth century CE. Often referred to as the Eastern Roman Empire, it was based in modern-day Turkey and spanned much of the Mediterranean. It was also a major mediaeval power that stood for a thousand years, finally collapsing in 1453 after the Fall of Constantinople, when the Ottoman Turkish conqueror Mehmed II captured the Byzantine capital, making it the capital of the Ottoman Empire instead. Constantinople has remained in Turkish hands ever since; however, these days it's known as Istanbul.[1]

Throughout the history of the Byzantine Empire, quite a number of its emperors died in unusual and sometimes spectacularly grisly ways. For instance, in the year 668, Constans II was murdered while in the bath—some accounts say with a knife, while others paint a picture of a rather more inventive (or perhaps forgetful) assassin and contend he was instead killed with a bucket. Then there's Constantine VI, who in 797 was overthrown by his own mother, Empress Irene, as part of her successful bid for power; she had Constantine blinded and let him rot in a prison cell until he died.

Worse still was what happened to the hated Andronikos I Komnenos. After being dethroned in 1185, he was tied to a post by an angry mob, who, over the course of three days, beat him to within an inch of his life, pulled out his hair and teeth, cut off one of his hands, gouged out one of his eyes, and threw boiling water in his face before hanging him upside down by his feet and tearing him to bits. The cruelty he had shown his people during his time as emperor was duly repaid, with interest.

More commonly, however, Byzantine emperors who died before their time were simply assassinated; assassination plots were a huge

1 But that's nobody's business but the Turks'.

part of the politics of the Byzantine Empire. Seven Byzantine emperors were assassinated, and a further seven were deposed and then mutilated in some way—sometimes blinded, sometimes castrated—which was just as effective as an assassination in terms of removing them from leadership, as Byzantines considered physical disfigurement enough to disqualify you from ruling.

Basil I avoided having his eyes gouged out and his tackle chopped off, but all the same he suffered a pretty nasty end that made him think he was the victim of an assassination attempt. He wasn't. Or maybe he was, and it was one of the most cunning assassinations history has ever seen. You be the judge.

Basil started out in life as a peasant, born in Macedonia in 811. Like any good Byzantine, he plotted and schemed and killed and murdered his way to power, firstly marrying the mistress of the reigning emperor Michael III as his ticket into the halls of power, before later being named co-emperor in 866. Sleeping his way to the top like this was a very clever bit of political moving and shaking, but he wasn't finished there. Not content to settle for co-emperor, Basil promptly arranged (can you guess?) the assassination of Michael III, and so became emperor in his own right thereafter. Most of the time, these Byzantine emperors really sound like Sith lords.

Basil I ruled the Byzantine Empire from 867 onwards, and his reign would ultimately last around two decades. He was generally very well liked and seemed to have done a good job, especially for someone who was born into the peasantry and never had a formal education or any military experience. He wrote a bunch of laws, built a bunch of buildings and, of course, fought a bunch of wars—although some of these didn't go too well: the Byzantine Empire lost control of Sicily to Muslim invaders thanks to some military blunders on Basil's part. You can't win 'em all!

All the same, the empire's power and influence spread under Basil, particularly across the Mediterranean, so broadly speaking he did an alright job and is generally counted among the better and more effective Byzantine emperors.

But then, in 886, death came for the 75-year-old Basil in a very unusual form: a deer. While Basil was on a hunt one day, a frenzied deer flashed past him; as it did, its antlers got tangled in Basil's belt. When the deer attempted to flee, Basil remained entangled and was dragged off through the forest along with it, and you can only imagine how the deer's panic must have risen. It would have been acutely aware of the mortifying breach of courtly etiquette it was making, dragging the ruler of the mightiest empire in Europe through a forest on its antlers!

Poor old Basil was dragged over *25 kilometres* through the forest by this deer, his imperial dignity somewhat diminished as he bonked off trees like a grey-haired learner-driver Tarzan, experiencing an all-natural holistic exfoliation treatment as he was dragged through bushes and bracken. He was eventually rescued by a servant who was able to catch up with him and free him from the deer's antlers by cutting his belt with a knife. You won't be surprised to learn that Basil wasn't in very good condition after this, and later died as a result of the injuries he had sustained. Though before he died, thankfully, he was able to reward the servant who had rescued him. For going above and beyond in seeking to aid his emperor, for his unquestionable devotion to his master by freeing Basil from the antlers of this murderous deer, the servant was rewarded with an immediate death sentence.

Basil suspected that this whole affair had been a murder plot, and thought that the servant who eventually caught up with him and cut him loose from the deer was in on it. Um, *how?* Did he *train* the deer to do this, Basil? Is that what you're suggesting—that he trained a deer to entangle elderly Byzantine emperors in its antlers, Basil? And, if he were in on it the whole time, why did he use his knife to cut the tangled belt free from the deer's antlers instead of just finishing the job himself? *Basil*?

Whatever the case, Basil deemed the servant as guilty in this supposed plot on his life as the deer had been, and one of his final orders as emperor was to have the poor bugger executed. Someone had to pay the blood price, and it wasn't going to be the murderous deer—who ended up being the real winner here by causing the death of two men for the price of one.

15

Jarl Sigurd the Mighty

Bitten by a Severed Head, 892

Harald Fairhair is said to have been the first king of Norway, unifying Vikings along the western coast of Scandinavia and establishing his new kingdom sometime around the 870s. After the Battle of Hafrsfjord, which—according to the Viking sagas—secured Harald's new kingdom, there were a fair few people who weren't too keen on the new king, and so they left Norway for greener pastures: specifically, the islands of Orkney off the northern coast of modern Scotland.

Harald wanted to keep an eye on these vanquished enemies, so he sent his relative Rognvald Eysteinsson over to Orkney to do what Vikings did best: raid and pillage, to keep those who had fled good and scared of their cousins back in Norway. Rognvald went one step further and actually conquered the Orkney Islands in Harald's name; he was duly elevated to the lofty position of jarl—an Old Norse term meaning 'chieftain', from which the modern English word 'earl' originates—and ruled Orkney on behalf of the Norwegian king.

A few years later, Rognvald decided that he'd had enough of Orkney and wanted to return to Norway.[1] Before leaving Orkney behind, Rognvald passed the title of jarl to his brother, Sigurd Eysteinsson, often referred to as Sigurd the Mighty. Sigurd, it seems, was an ambitious jarl, and he sought to expand his power and sphere of influence beyond Orkney. So he, too, got on with what Vikings did best: raiding and pillaging the Scottish—or Pictish, at the time—coastline, and terrorising the Picts who lived there. The Vikings already had a long and proud history of giving the British Isles what historians informally refer to as 'the business', and Sigurd enthusiastically upheld this tradition. Like his brother, he also went further than raiding and pillaging: he conquered large areas under Pictish control, places we now call Caithness and Sutherland in northern Scotland.

So successful were Sigurd's conquests that he earned himself the moniker 'the mighty', which, out of all of the epithets available, is right up there alongside other bangers such as 'the great' or 'the magnificent'. It's certainly better than 'the bucktoothed', which belonged to the man who ended up killing Sigurd—*after* Sigurd had killed *him*.

Hang on, what? Let's back up and explain things properly.

---

1 Perhaps he was pining for the fjords.

After conquering much of the Scottish Highlands, Sigurd ruled his domains for almost two decades, until around 892. He seemed to have been keen to keep expanding his territories, however, because at the time of his death, he was still fighting to conquer more lands. While campaigning against the Picts, he came up against a local leader known as Máel Brigte the Bucktoothed, whose prominent teeth would be Sigurd's downfall—in a way that nine out of ten dentists agree they didn't see coming.

In seeking to conquer Máel Brigte's territory, Sigurd challenged him to a 40-a-side pitched battle. Máel Brigte agreed, and when he assembled with his forces, he was probably more than a little pissed off to find that the perfidious Sigurd had brought not 40 but *80* men with him. Sigurd and his numerically superior Vikings absolutely wiped the floor with the unhappy Picts, and after his rousing victory Sigurd himself decapitated Máel Brigte and took his severed head, buckteeth and all, as a grisly trophy. He strapped the head to his saddle for all to see as he rode off proudly, congratulating himself on another fine day's work.

But we all know that cheaters never prosper,[2] and Sigurd was about to experience some laser-guided instant karma. As he rode off with Máel Brigte's head bouncing along beside him, one of Máel Brigte's aforementioned buckteeth lacerated Sigurd's leg, deep enough to draw blood. Later, the wound became infected, and it festered into a full-blown case of septicaemia—and with mediaeval medicine being

2 Except for Diego Maradona. He ended up doing alright.

what it was, Sigurd died shortly thereafter. It's not like he could have gone to an apothecary and asked for a tincture of penicillin; the best he could have hoped for was a handful of leeches and a poultice made of goat shit.

And lo, so it was that Sigurd the Mighty slew Máel Brigte the Bucktoothed, but this killing lacked honour, as Sigurd achieved it through false-hearted treachery. Conversely, Máel Brigte's posthumous killing of Sigurd was . . . well . . . no, it *also* lacked honour, in truth. There's not much glory in accidentally biting a foe to death after you yourself have been killed, but on the other hand it also kind of feels like the best that someone known as 'the bucktoothed' could hope for.

16

Duke Godfrey IV of Lower Lorraine

Assassinated while Having a Shit, 1076

The French duke Godfrey IV of Lower Lorraine, often referred to as Godfrey the Hunchback, had his rule cut short in 1076 by—so the story goes—a deadly trip to the dunny.

There are plenty of stories of nobles dying on the bog: George II of Great Britain died of an aortic dissection after busting a grumpy, while Edmund Ironside of England and Wenceslaus III of Bohemia are said to have been assassinated while punishing the proverbial porcelain. Although, it must be said that these last two might be apocryphal, and plenty of historians think that these stories are a load of, well, the last thing Edmund and Wenceslaus are said to have been dealing with when they were assassinated.

Godfrey's story, however, is much more reliably sourced. While historians argue over where he was killed in *broad* terms—Utrecht, Antwerp, or Vlaardingen—in *specific* terms, everyone agrees: it was on the thunderbox.

Godfrey was the husband of Matilda of Tuscany, one of the most important figures in Italian mediaeval history, although apparently the two didn't get on all that well. Godfrey spent his career as a duke doing the thing that good dukes do: fighting on behalf of his liege lord, Holy Roman Emperor Henry IV.

Godfrey obviously made some powerful enemies while doing this, because in 1076 someone hired an assassin to kill him. And, reprehensibly, this assassin struck Godfrey in a place that should be sacred and sacrosanct. A place you can retreat to when the world and its worries become too much, where you can relax and reflect in peace and, if you're in a literary mood, read the back of a shampoo bottle or two: the toilet.

Now, this assassin didn't kick in the door and stab the defenceless Godfrey in the chest while he was pinching off a ferocious turd, oh no. The assassin is said to have *hidden in the privy itself*, in the chute in which the foul effluent would be deposited. Despite his evil intentions, you'll agree that this was an assassin who was truly dedicated to his craft.

After lying in wait and finally finding himself eye to eye with Godfrey's arse winking at him atop the dunny hole, the assassin struck: he fatally stabbed Godfrey from below with what was, presumably, a spear. This makes sense, as the assassin probably didn't want to get *too* close. What did you expect—that he was going to wipe Godfrey's bum for him as well?

Poor old Godfrey died of his wounds. What a crap way to go: you think you're going to be murdering a brown snake, but in the end it's *you* who gets murdered instead.

His death upset the local power balance a little bit, but Henry IV stepped in to smooth things over. History marched on, leaving Godfrey as one of the few confirmed notable deaths to have taken place on the toilet. However, Godfrey certainly isn't the most famous person to have passed away like this. If we're going to talk about kings and dukes dying on the toilet, we'd better not forget the most famous king of all to die atop a porcelain throne: the King of Rock and Roll, Elvis Presley.

17

The *White Ship* Disaster

When 300 English Nobles Drowned at Sea, 1120

The years between 1135 and 1153 are referred to in English history as 'The Anarchy'. A succession crisis kicked off when King Henry I of England, son of the famous William the Conqueror and his wife Matilda of Flanders,[1] died without a legitimate male heir.

According to the twelfth-century English historian Henry of Huntingdon, King Henry I died after eating too many lampreys, which were considered a delicacy back then. As strange as it may seem that people ever thought slimy, eel-like fish with Sarlacc-like mouths

1 Matilda No. 1. You'll see why we're enumerating them in a moment.

were gourmet eating, don't forget that England is a country famous for culinary offerings such as black pudding, which is a sausage made by mixing pig's blood and oatmeal. Lampreys don't seem so bad now, do they?

In any case, after Henry's lamprey-induced death, his daughter Matilda[2] was challenged for the English throne by her cousin, William the Conqueror's grandson Stephen of Blois. Stephen's claim on the English throne was complex and multifaceted, but at its core it relied on the argument that Matilda had a fundamental lack of three key things that he felt the job required: a penis, a testicle, and another testicle to keep the first one company.

Matilda and Stephen scrapping over the English throne brought about The Anarchy, a period of great political turmoil across the entire kingdom that was essentially a civil war. As is generally the case in situations like this, the common folk of England suffered the worst of it: famine, lawlessness, displacement, death . . . all of these could have been avoided with a smooth succession process, something that Henry didn't seem to have prepared for before gorging himself to death on mucous-covered jawless fish.

But he did, in fact, prepare for it! Back in 1103, his wife Queen Matilda of Scotland[3] had given birth to a son, William Adelin, who up until the affair of the *White Ship* was heir to the English throne. A

2 Matilda No. 2. We're barely warming up.

3 Matilda No. 3. She seems to have named her daughter (Matilda No. 2) after herself.

year after his marriage to Matilda of Anjou,[4] William Adelin drowned on the *White Ship* in 1120, and his death precipitated the succession crisis of 1135 and the consequent Anarchy. Then again, maybe England dodged a bullet. William's altogether thoughtlessly timed death, which would plunge the kingdom into chaos, is perhaps an indication of bad judgement—hardly a desirable trait in a king.

In late November 1120, King Henry I was over in his homeland of Normandy, along the north coast of what is today France. Despite being king of England, Henry was still in charge of Normandy, and he had to head back there now and again to keep his blasted barons in line, as they were fully committed to the age-old pastime of the European mediaeval baron: making life as difficult as possible for his lord. Henry prudently bought off the worst of them, mercilessly crushed the rest, and made ready to return to England.

Henry had brought quite a retinue across the English Channel with him, including his son and heir William Adelin, his illegitimate children Richard of Lincoln and Matilda FitzRoy,[5] and countless other English royals and nobles besides. They were slated to return to England after Henry, aboard a vessel called the *White Ship*.

---

4 Matilda No. 4. Unrelated to all of the other Matildas—until she married William, that is.

5 Matilda No. 5. Not only was Henry's wife named Matilda (No. 3), not only did he have a daughter named Matilda (No. 2), but he also named the daughter he had with *another* woman Matilda. Don't forget that his mum, William the Conqueror's wife, was *also* named Matilda (No. 1), as was his daughter-in-law (No. 4).

The story goes, however, that before setting sail, William Adelin was in the mood for merriment, and so he ordered a vast quantity of wine to be provided not just to his aristocratic associates but also to the ship's crew. Around 300 people were aboard as it prepared to set sail, although one ultimately very fortunate passenger decided to disembark from the ship before it left because of a particularly nasty bout of diarrhoea. As the *White Ship* would go on to sink and kill almost everyone aboard her, it's fair to say that there's not a single person in history who had a luckier case of the squirts—and, as will be clear in due course, not just because it saved his life.

The *White Ship* was a state-of-the-art vessel, sleek and speedy. Knowing this, William Adelin and his entourage of drunken party animals urged the equally drunken crew to get the wind in her sails and get her over to England at full speed, thinking it would be a fine thing to beat Henry I back there. The pissed-up sailors put their backs into it, and before long the *White Ship* went whizzing across the waves—and straight into a submerged rock.

After striking the rock, the ship continued to make blisteringly fast progress, although this time on a slightly different trajectory: approximately 90 degrees downward along the Y-axis, which is very rarely the desired direction for a seagoing vessel. As she filled with water and sank, the ship took almost every single person aboard down with her. The only reported survivor was a butcher named Berold of Rouen, who made it out alive by holding on to the rock that the ship had run into until he was later rescued.

It wasn't just Henry's son and heir plus two of his other kids who drowned with the sinking of the *White Ship*. Also aboard were members of the royal household and the clergy, as well as a great many English and Norman noblemen and noblewomen. One such noblewoman was a woman named . . . yes, Matilda,[6] who was the sister of that lucky diarrhoea-stricken fellow who had left the *White Ship* at the last moment.

And the name of the man who departed the ship prematurely, squirting like a country goose as he did so? It was none other than, believe it or not, Stephen of Blois. After narrowly avoiding death on the *White Ship* thanks to his overpowering need to spray-paint the garderobe, fifteen years later Stephen was able to seize the very throne that the *White Ship* helped to vacate!

Stephen went on to rule England—in name, at least—throughout The Anarchy, defending his claim from Henry's daughter Matilda until 1153, when peace was finally negotiated and his rule confirmed . . . for the moment. Stephen really didn't make the most of this peace, promptly dying the very next year. For that brief period, though, he was able to rule England in relative tranquillity, alongside his wife.

Whose name was . . .

Matilda.[7]

6 Matilda No. 6. Evidently they didn't have baby name books back then.

7 Matilda No. 7. At last, we can rest.

18

The Erfurt Latrine Disaster

When 60 German Nobles Drowned in Excrement, 1184

Back in the late twelfth century, land feuds were a very popular way for nobles in the Holy Roman Empire to pass the time. In 1184, one land feud in particular got so heated that the Holy Roman Emperor's son, Henry of Hohenstaufen, had to intervene. To settle the dispute, Henry invited those involved in the feud—along with a fair few others who just wanted to come along and enjoy the show—to Petersberg Citadel in Erfurt to talk it all through. Unfortunately for everyone involved, mediaeval building codes have never been noted for their rigour, and Petersberg Citadel lacked a certain structural integrity that the entitled and enthusiastically litigious people of the 21st century tend to take for granted. As this horde of excited nobles assembled, it proved to be too much for the floor to bear, with some pretty shitty results for all concerned.

The trouble initially arose when a minor noble named Conrad became the Archbishop of Mainz in 1183. He immediately claimed some land that encroached into the territory of Ludwig III, the Landgrave of Thuringia. This caused Ludwig to arc up, ready to defend what was his from this contemptible priest, kicking off the land feud that would ultimately lead to the Erfurt Latrine Disaster.

Land feuds in the Holy Roman Empire were, to put it mildly, *extremely* common. If you're wondering just how common, have a look at any twelfth-century map of the Holy Roman Empire. Because of the constantly shifting internal divisions, these maps look like a kindergartener's finger painting—but a *bad* one that you'd be too embarrassed to put on the fridge, in case the neighbours saw it. They look like a drunk person convinced themselves they would be able to hand-draw one of those magic eye puzzles you used to do when you were a kid. They look like someone broke a stained-glass window and then tried to put it back together with superglue, hoping no one would notice.

In any case, Conrad and Ludwig had evidently looked at a map and decided that it wasn't sufficiently chaotic, because they fully leaned into a wider conflict within the Holy Roman Empire between feudal lords and church landholders, and went after each other like little kids fighting over the good LEGO pieces. And, just like little kids, they ultimately needed an adult to step in and resolve the conflict for them, so Holy Roman Emperor Frederick Barbarossa sent off his eighteen-year-old son to sort it all out.

Henry of Hohenstaufen—later Henry VI of the Holy Roman Empire—arrived in the Thuringian town of Erfurt on 25 July 1184 with the intention of holding a *Hoftag*: an informal assembly where local leaders could air grievances or resolve disputes. Invitations had been sent out to nobles in the surrounding regions to attend in case they had any issues they may want dealt with, but most came just because they wanted to see Ludwig and Conrad get stuck into each other. Land feuds were great fun for the average noble lord: nothing like a bit of mediaeval *Jerry Springer* to take your mind off the difficult task of finding new and inventive ways to oppress and exploit the peasantry.

Over a hundred of them arrived in Erfurt for this *Hoftag*, held on the first floor[1] of St Peter's Church in the Petersberg Citadel. They packed themselves in like overdressed sardines, keen to watch the

1 Or the second floor, for those readers in China, Japan, Indonesia and the Americas (except, interestingly, people in Brazil, Mexico, and Argentina, who understand the concept of a ground floor).

drama unfold, while Henry himself took his position at the head of the room, keen to fold up the drama.

But now, it's time for a quick toilet break.

Going to the toilet during the European mediaeval period could be a harrowing experience. A socially conscious commoner would head to the outskirts of town and squat over a ditch to blast out a turd, while a commoner with fewer inhibitions would just nip down the nearest alleyway. Incidentally, for reasons that mystify scholars to this very day, mediaeval towns didn't smell very nice.

Rather than squat in an alleyway, those of the upper social strata would often use personal chamber pots in the comfort and privacy of their own homes. All the same, this resulted in an identical outcome to the disgusting deposits of the alleyway peasant, as in general these chamber pots were emptied straight out of the nearest window, to the great peril of anyone squatting in the alleyway below.

Larger towns and cities with a river running through them would often build toilets into their bridges so you could conveniently punch one out straight into the water below and make it the problem of someone else, far downstream. In addition to these river dunnies, larger settlements would often build communal latrines over a very sophisticated piece of human technology: a big hole in the ground.

These cesspits, as they were called, were a testament to human ingenuity and an attestation of our ability to tackle and solve the problems that face us. The remarkably inventive approach we took with many mediaeval sewage systems illustrates a time-honoured guiding principle of our approach to problem-solving as humans: *out of sight, out of mind*.[2] After all, we've been burying our turds since the dawn of humanity, so why stop now?

Cesspits like this were usually constructed in one of two ways. Some were built to be emptied, in which case they were readily accessible and usually a little smaller. A person with the world's most unenviable but highly necessary job would, at regular intervals, come along and take away all of the malodorous waste, and take it . . . elsewhere, thank you very much.

Conversely, the alternative was to never empty the cesspit. This type of pit was dug, like, *really* deep, in order to make it the problem of some unlucky bastard in the future once it finally filled up. This illustrates another of our very effective problem-solving methods: just kick the can down the road and trust that someone else will deal with it at some point. No matter if we shit into a river, a small hole, a big hole, or even a modern flushing toilet today, the objective has always been the same: to make sure that our business becomes, in the end, someone else's business.

Anyway, a deeply dug cesspit and its accompanying latrines serviced St Peter's Church, and the pit was old enough to already be nice and full of years and years' worth of the generous deposits people had made into it. And, as it so happened, the latrines under which this cesspit had been dug were themselves located right under the deanery where, on 26 July 1184, a hundred or so nobles were crammed

2 Given the stink of a cesspit, it's lucky the saying isn't 'out of *smell*, out of mind'.

together, eagerly awaiting the arrival of Henry, the beginning of the *Hoftag*, and the fiery political drama that would unfold.

As previously mentioned, mediaeval building standards can be diplomatically described as somewhat lacklustre. The timber floor, held up by beams that were who knows how old, couldn't support the combined weight of all of the nobles who had piled inside the church. The wood might have been rotten, it might have been in disrepair, who knows—but what we do know is that sometime after the *Hoftag* got underway, the entire floor collapsed with a splintering crash.

There was good news and bad news for the nobles who plunged down through the hole made by these unplanned renovations. The good news was that they had a softer landing than they might have expected, as the impact of the collapsed floor resulted in the latrines beneath also giving way. This meant that rather than going *splat* as they fell onto the hard floor of the latrines, the nobles instead went *splash* as they fell into the deep cesspit filled with many years' worth of excreta.

The bad news, however, was that they fell into a deep cesspit filled with many years' worth of excreta. Sixty of these mediaeval lords never made it back out, either: they actually drowned in this foul, stinking, liquified faecal marinade.

Fortunately for our three main characters, though, they avoided this grim fate and managed to survive the entire ordeal. Ludwig was unlucky enough to be among the nobles who fell in, but he wasn't as unlucky as the 60 who never got back out, as he ultimately escaped from the putrescent waste below. What's truly remarkable about this is that, although he suffered cuts and scratches in the fall, somehow they didn't get infected after he scrabbled his way out of the turd soup. He and the rest of the nobles who made it out were rescued as people converged on the church to help drag these putrid lords out of the cesspit. Ludwig survived to tell the tale, or, more likely, survived to *not* tell the tale.

As for Henry and Conrad, they were among the very few truly lucky ones. Henry had taken his place at the head of the room for the *Hoftag*, in a small stone alcove built into the wall of the church itself. Conrad was standing next to Henry when the floor collapsed (perhaps it had been his turn to address the *Hoftag*), which meant that when the floor gave out they were both safe with stone underfoot, perched above the catastrophe like a pair of reluctant synchronised divers.

But while they were safe from the carnage in the cesspit, they were still stuck in this alcove while a hundred or so noblemen desperately floundered about below. The future Holy Roman Emperor and his archbishop had to wait like two cats stuck up a tree until some Erfurt locals found ladders and set them up on the broken floor, allowing them to safely descend. As soon as he was finally rescued, Henry didn't hang about: he left Erfurt immediately, evidently very ready to put as much distance as possible between himself and the horrors he'd just witnessed.

This meant that the issue that gave rise to the Erfurt Latrine Disaster—the land feud between Ludwig and Conrad—was never resolved. Henry left Erfurt without ever making a decision on the dispute, and it really didn't seem to come up all that much afterwards. It must have become a rather awkward topic of conversation, for some reason. Nonetheless, this disaster does offer a useful piece of advice for anyone attempting to succeed in the world of high-level conflict resolution: when presented with a particularly knotty problem, just have 60 or so nobles drown in a pit of liquid shit while you're weighing things up, and no one will bother you about the issue ever again.

19

Caliph al-Musta'sim

Trampled to Death while Rolled Up in a Rug, 1258

The last caliph of the Baghdad-based Abbasid Caliphate, al-Musta'sim bi-llāh, is said to have suffered a highly unusual death at the hands of the Mongol conquerors who sacked his capital in 1258. After capturing the Abbasid capital, Mongol leader Hulagu Khan took time out of his busy razing, pillaging, and massacring schedule to oversee the execution of his vanquished foe in Baghdad, choosing to employ a method that showcased not only the Mongols' world-famous mastery of horses but also Hulagu's avant-garde approach to interior design.

At its peak, the Abbasid Caliphate ruled an empire that stretched from Tunisia to Turkmenistan; it was one of the most advanced and enlightened mediaeval civilisations on the planet. Its legendary House of Wisdom—also known as the Grand Library of Baghdad—was one of the world's largest and most important places of learning, and the empire itself was a multiethnic and religiously tolerant realm that powered the Golden Age of Islam from the eighth to the thirteenth centuries. Unfortunately, this Golden Age came to an end, along with al-Musta'sim's life, when the Mongols turned up, uninvited, in Baghdad in 1258.

Before this, al-Musta'sim wasn't, to put it as tactfully as possible, the best caliph the Abbasids had ever seen. Born in 1213 and taking the throne in 1242 after the death of his old man, al-Mustansir, al-Musta'sim seemed to be in over his head even at the best of times. He was indecisive and ineffectual, and had a bad habit of making promises he couldn't keep. Diplomatic posturing, empty threats and a near-total lack of readiness for a Mongol invasion were the hallmarks of al-Musta'sim's reign; it's hardly the historical legacy for which anyone would hope, but then again, it may not have actually been completely his fault.

Before his 1258 invasion, Mongol leader Hulagu Khan got in touch with al-Musta'sim, demanding his surrender. Hulagu warned the caliph that the Mongols had come to chew bubblegum and raze cities; as bubblegum wouldn't be invented until 1928, this left Hulagu with precious few options. Baghdad was in the Mongol crosshairs.

However, al-Musta'sim's grand vizier, Ibn al-Alkami, insisted that the Mongols weren't a threat. And if they were, the Abbasids could repel them. And if they couldn't, they had the option to call in allies who could. And if those allies couldn't . . . well, look, let's not worry about that too much, shall we?

Ibn al-Alkami may have been ill-informed, he may have been corrupt, or he may have just been an idiot. Whatever the case, al-Musta'sim firmly rebuffed Hulagu's threats, firmly refused to secure the city by improving its defences, and firmly failed to mobilise regional allies to help fight the oncoming Mongol horde. Imagine his surprise when Hulagu arrived with a small group of friends—out of nowhere, 100,000 Mongol-led troops were suddenly knocking on Baghdad's door, ready to put the city to the fire and the sword.

Mongolia is famous for many things: its breathtaking, rugged mountain vistas; the exceptional quality of its cashmere wool; the, ah . . . *intriguing* sound of its throat-singers. It's also very famous, historically speaking, for producing some of the fiercest and most bloodthirsty warriors the world has ever seen—warriors who weren't, on the whole, accustomed to defeat. And in 1258, they were poised to attack a city whose leader had, in his infinite wisdom, left it largely undefended.

The 1258 Siege of Baghdad resulted in not just the near-total destruction of the city, but also, just for good measure, the near-total massacre of its population: estimates of the death toll range from 200,000 to as many as two million. The Mongols slaughtered people indiscriminately, burning buildings and books as they went. It's said that the Tigris River ran red with blood due to the depredations of the invading army, and even today Baghdad has never fully recovered its former splendour and glory.

As the devastation unfolded, al-Musta'sim was taken prisoner by Hulagu and forced to watch as his city was burned and his people were murdered. However, when it came to the murder of al-Musta'sim himself, things weren't so simple for the Mongols.

Apparently,[1] the Mongols had a strict taboo on the spilling of royal blood. They believed that if royal blood touched the ground, it would cause all manner of catastrophe and calamity brought on by divine wrath, and so it wasn't as simple as lopping off al-Musta'sim's head and calling it a day. Still, al-Musta'sim had to die, that much was clear. Bloodless execution methods were readily available in the mediaeval era, even if they didn't have all of the marvellous modern conveniences of today's world, such as electric chairs and lethal injections. They could have hanged al-Musta'sim, for instance, but no: Hulagu decided on a different tack.

In an inventive effort to ensure that the royal blood of the last Abbasid caliph wouldn't touch the ground and provoke the anger of the gods, al-Musta'sim was taken by the Mongols and rolled up in a rug, before a horde of Mongol horsemen trampled him to death under hoof.

---

1 'Apparently' in this context is doing a lot of heavy lifting as a cowardly way to express the idea that not all historical sources agree on what's written next.

And so ended the Golden Age of Islam, the supremacy of Baghdad as the world's most learned city, and the life of the last Abbasid caliph. The rug duly prevented any royal blood from touching the ground; with this manner of execution, the Mongols really did give al-Musta'sim the red-carpet treatment.

20

King Charles the Bad

Burned to a Crisp on Doctor's Orders, 1387

As Charles the Bad would probably tell you, there are plenty of historical epithets that you'd rather avoid having. There's Selim the Drunk, for instance, or Piero the Unfortunate; in the thirteenth century, a Bulgarian peasant leader had the bad luck to be labelled Ivaylo the Cabbage. Charles the Bad is only one letter away from another less-than-ideal epithet: Charles the Bald,[1] a ninth-century Frankish emperor and grandson of the legendary Charlemagne, who

1 Whom you may remember from an earlier chapter: he was one of the lucky French kings who *didn't* die after bonking his head on a doorframe.

was apparently called 'the bald' because he had a thick, rich head of hair. Lucky for him. In any case, it certainly gets worse than Charles the Bad: Ivan the Terrible immediately comes to mind. Sure, Charles is bad, but at least he's not *terrible*.

Born in 1332, Charles the Bad—Charles II of Navarre, officially speaking—took the throne as the king of Navarre in 1349, ruling a tiny kingdom in the Pyrenees mountains that is part of modern-day Spain. He was known as 'the Bad' not because he was a Charles of particularly poor quality, the sort whom you might return in the hope of an exchange or refund, but because he was constantly plotting, planning, scheming and double-crossing. Maybe they couldn't fit Charles the Really Shifty Bastard on his driver's licence.

Charles was a thoroughly dishonest king. He made a habit of betraying people, always looking for a way to advance his kingdom's agenda at the expense of others, against the backdrop of the Hundred Years' War fought between England and France. He would switch sides back and forth, depending on which way the wind was blowing and who was making him the better offer at the time. Charles the Bad, as you might expect based on his very well-chosen epithet, really didn't have any scruples whatsoever.

Initially, Charles held a bunch of territory in France but lost most of it after it was revealed that he was plotting with the English against the French during the Hundred Years' War. John II, the French king, found out about this treachery and didn't waste a second: he had Charles arrested and stripped of many of his French titles. This didn't stop Charles, though. He escaped from prison and continued wheeling and dealing behind the scenes with other French nobles, before steadily betraying each and every one of them in turn.

However, it all came a cropper in 1378, when his plan to poison the new French king, Charles V, came to light. This was the beginning of the end for our crafty friend, who had put far too many noses out of joint to get out of this situation.

The French marched on Charles the Bad's remaining French holdings. Charles appealed to the English for aid, and the English swiftly sent reinforcements . . . who promptly seized the lands that the French hadn't, giving Charles a taste of his own medicine with a very neat little double-cross.

In his affairs on the other side of the Pyrenees, in the Spanish world, it was more of the same. In the 1360s, the Spanish kingdoms of Castile and Aragon had gone to war with one another, and Charles had allied himself with Castile—before, of course, stabbing the Castilians in the back and switching to Aragon. This proved to be a bad move, as Castile eventually invaded Navarre and absolutely rolled Charles, forcing him to surrender and lose even *more* of his lands.

From go to whoa, Charles the Bad was . . . well, bad. His career as king was filled with bad-faith deals, betrayals, and back-stabbings, and the best part is that they brought him no benefit at all. He went from being a powerful king with extensive French holdings to a humbled, humiliated laughing-stock whom no one trusted even a little bit. Maybe 'the Bad' actually does mean 'poor quality' after all, because he certainly wasn't very *good* at being a king.

Ultimately, after a lifetime of plots, schemes, and poorly executed intrigues, the death of Charles the Bad in 1387 was widely celebrated, especially once news of its very gruesome nature spread.

In his old age, Charles became very unwell: he was full of all sorts of exciting diseases that rendered him so weak he was hardly able to move. The court physician examined the king and ordered that he be kept very warm at all times. Perhaps the physician should have been more specific in exactly *how* warm because, as it turns out, his orders were followed a little too closely.

To make sure that the king stayed nice and toasty, the physician decided that Charles should be wrapped tightly in strips of linen that had been soaked in brandy. You'd be forgiven for thinking that this was a strange way to keep someone warm—how about just using a blanket or something?—but the linen-drenched-in-brandy approach did end up working very well: thanks to either a nearby candle or some hot coals, the alcohol-soaked cloth the king had been wrapped in immediately caught fire. Just as the doctor ordered, Charles was kept very warm indeed for the rest of his life, as he burned to a crisp and died.

Not many people mourned the death of Charles the Bad. If anything, many saw it as his just deserts: his comeuppance for all of his betrayals and backstabbing. It certainly casts a new light on the phrase 'liar, liar, pants on fire', doesn't it? Charles the Bad was so dishonest that in his case it ended up being 'liar, liar, *whole body* on fire'.

21

Emperor Humāyūn

Fell Down Some Stairs while Praying, 1556

In 1530, the mighty Babur, founder of the Mughal Empire, died and was replaced as emperor by his son Humāyūn. Born in 1508 as Nasir al-Din Muhammad, Humāyūn came to power at the young age of 22. In the years to come, he would spend more time fighting to hold onto or retake the imperial throne than actually sitting on it.

At its peak, the Mughal Empire stretched from modern-day Afghanistan across the Indian subcontinent to Bangladesh; but when Humāyūn took the throne, it was a fair bit smaller, running along the southern Himalayas to span the northern part of modern India. Further, politically speaking, the realm he inherited from his old man was unstable and fractured, with much of it not under firm imperial control.

Humāyūn spent the first decade of his rule trying to unify and consolidate his empire, travelling from one end of it to the other to put down revolts here or negotiate with nobles there. Eventually this all became too much for him, and he was overthrown by a general named Sher Shah Suri, who also grew to become a very important figure in Mughal history. A brilliant strategist, Sher Shah reformed the Mughal Empire, introduced the rupee as its currency, and in just five years did a lot of what Humāyūn couldn't in terms of consolidating power over his realm.

Humāyūn was sent to Persia in exile by Sher Shah, but he never gave up hope of reclaiming his empire. In time, Humāyūn gathered what forces he could and slowly but surely conquered his way back into the Mughal Empire. This effort was aided when Sher Shah Suri very obligingly died in 1545, with the resulting political fallout only making a campaign of reconquest easier for Humāyūn. In the wake of Sher Shah Suri's death, Humāyūn captured territories in modern-day Afghanistan and Pakistan, and then steadily worked his way into and across India.

At last, by 1555, Humāyūn had regained control of the Mughal Empire. Sher Shah Suri's heirs were too busy fighting each other to stand up to Humāyūn, and his capture of Delhi finalised his reclamation of the empire. Unfortunately, though—as you might have already guessed—it wasn't to last, because around six months after taking the throne back, Humāyūn was dead.

Assassinated by one of Sher Shah's belligerent heirs, perhaps? Or was he killed while putting down a rebellion or a revolt that challenged his rule?

Nope. He fell down some stairs.

Humāyūn was a devout Muslim, and as such he diligently prayed at appointed times five times a day. Such was his devotion to his faith that as soon as one of these appointed prayer times came, Humāyūn would firstly drop whatever he was doing—no matter how important—then secondly drop to his knees and pray. Sadly for him, however, one day the *adhan*—the call to prayer—came when he was walking down a flight of stairs from a library, with an armful of books. Nonetheless, when Humāyūn heard the *adhan*, he immediately dropped his books and went to kneel down in prayer, right there on the stairs.

This didn't work out so well for the ill-fated Humāyūn. Kneeling down on stairs is a tricky thing to do at the best of times; rushing about with an armload of books isn't going to make it any easier, nor is doing all this while also wearing the stately robes of a Mughal emperor. As Humāyūn knelt, his foot got caught in his robes and he lost his balance, toppled over, and fell down the stairs. As he bounced from stair to stair, books flying everywhere, he cracked his head open on one of them and, sadly, that was it for him. He never recovered: after being taken away for rest and treatment, he died three days after the accident.

There was a silver lining here.[1] Humāyūn's death made way for his son, Akbar, to take the throne, and in time Akbar would go on to be

1 Not that it would have been much comfort to the dead Humāyūn, mind you.

known as Akbar the Great, one of the greatest rulers in Indian history. During his reign, the power of the Mughal Empire was entrenched as a vast, immensely wealthy, culturally integrated, and quite liberal realm. So, ultimately, Humāyūn's death wasn't in vain when it came to the success and prosperity of the empire for which he had fought so hard. Those stairs must have had the empire's best interests at heart.

22

Hans Staininger

Fell Down Some Stairs while Bearded, 1567

Hans Staininger, the *bürgermeister* (mayor) of the town of Braunau am Inn, had a long and magnificent beard that was said to be 2 metres in length. It wasn't just the pride of Staininger, but also the pride of the town at large: it is, perhaps, the second-most-famous example of facial hair associated with Braunau am Inn.[1]

Staininger was born around 1508 in the nearby town of Pfarrkirchen, which at the time was part of the Kingdom of Bavaria,

1 Today, Braunau am Inn is internationally famous—or infamous, rather—as the birthplace of a certain vegetarian failed painter who had *much* less facial hair than Staininger.

as indeed was Braunau back in the sixteenth century. At some point, he moved to Braunau, and was elected as *bürgermeister* no fewer than six times—his popularity doubtless spurred on by his spectacular whiskers.

The talk of the town, Staininger's beard was as splendid as it was enormously long and luxurious. Staininger used to roll it up and stow it safely in a large bag-like pocket before he strode about Braunau, presumably dividing the population of the town between endless admiration and seething envy. After all, quite aside from granting you a comely visage, a 2-metre-long beard can confer a great many useful advantages upon its bearer:

1. **Human windsock:** Stand in the wind and allow passers-by to conveniently observe its current speed and direction.
2. **Nature's broom:** Use your beard to keep the streets clean, effortlessly sweeping them as you stroll along on your daily constitutional.
3. **Living scarf:** Keep yourself safe from the chill of wintry weather by wrapping your beard around your neck as a scarf.
4. **Emergency pillow:** When struck by the need for a quick nap, roll up your beard and use it as a soft and bushy pillow.
5. **Instant wig:** Balding? Not anymore—hide your shameful secret under the abundant locks that grow from your face. It's cheaper than plugs!
6. **Impromptu curtain:** Avoid being woken up by the blinding light of an early dawn by hanging your beard across an east-facing window.

7. **Portable hammock:** String your beard between two trees and luxuriate in the comfort of your own personal hammock.
8. **Stationery organiser:** Store your pens and pencils within your beard, turning it into a mobile office-supply holder.
9. **Hiding place:** Become a hide-and-seek champion by concealing yourself behind your own beard. It's the last place they'll look!
10. **Bird's nest:** Provide a cosy, predator-free environment for small birds and animals in your voluminous beard.

As you can see, a 2-metre-long beard is not only immensely attractive but also extremely practical, with a multitude of handy, everyday functions. Delight your friends and confound your enemies: consider growing a 2-metre-long beard today.

Be aware, though, that a 2-metre-long beard comes with certain dangers, as Staininger himself once—and only once—emphatically demonstrated.

On the night of 28 September 1567, a fire broke out in Braunau. As a devoted *bürgermeister*, when Staininger heard the alarm being raised he leaped from his bed and rushed down the stairs of his home to provide assistance. Unfortunately, his journey down the stairs was involuntarily accelerated by his beard. Failing to tuck it away safely beforehand, Staininger trod on the end of his beard as he began descending the staircase, tripped over, and broke his neck as he fell down the stairs. Live by the beard, die by the beard: Staininger is one of the very few people throughout history to have been killed by their own facial hair.

Staininger was interred in the local cemetery, and today you can still go and visit his grave in Braunau. His beard, however, was cut off before he was buried, and after being passed down as a family heirloom for generations, it was finally bequeathed to the Bezirksmuseum Herzogsburg in Braunau am Inn, where it remains on display, in all its glory, to this very day.

23

Tycho Brahe

Died after Not Going to the Toilet Because He Thought It Might Be a Bit Rude, 1601

Tycho Brahe was a very famous Danish astronomer, known to history for his amazingly accurate astronomical observations throughout the back half of the sixteenth century. What is particularly remarkable about Brahe and his astronomical work is that he didn't use telescopes, and for a very good reason: they wouldn't be invented until after his death.[1]

1 The first patent application for a telescope was submitted in 1608 by a Dutch-German spectacle-maker named Hans Lipperhey. The patent office denied the application, in what could be described as a very short-sighted move. Perhaps they needed a pair of Lipperhey's spectacles.

All the same, even without the telescope, Brahe secured a legacy as one of the greatest astronomers in history, getting out there and just rawdogging the night sky.

This isn't the only thing that's remarkable about Brahe, however: he died as a result of his own determined politeness, which isn't a cause of death you see on all that many death certificates.

Born in 1546, Brahe was a scion of the Danish nobility and enjoyed excellent political connections and a first-rate education, developing an interest in astronomy while studying law at the University of Copenhagen. After witnessing—and being amazed by—a solar eclipse in 1560, Brahe eventually left behind his law degree after getting into astronomy, and around this time he also left behind his nose after getting into a duel.

In 1566, Brahe had a heated argument with another Danish nobleman, Manderup Parsberg, about who was the better mathematician. Brahe may or may not have been the better mathematician, but he certainly wasn't the better swordsman: when the argument escalated into a duel, Parsberg was able to slice off Brahe's nose. For the rest of his life, Brahe wore a prosthetic nose made of brass; he carried a little pot of glue with him wherever he went, in readiness for any particularly violent sneezes.[2]

Brahe's scientific career was groundbreaking. It changed humanity's understanding of the heavens and lay the groundwork for future

2 This sounds like a cheap gag, but it's not. Brahe really did carry a bit of glue around with him everywhere in case he had to reattach his brass nose when it fell off.

generations of famous astronomers. With the backing of the Danish king, Frederick II, Brahe built an observatory called Uraniborg on the island of Hven and began to meticulously observe the night sky, tracking and recording the changing positions of stars and planets. Uraniborg was one of the most advanced astronomical and research facilities on the face of the planet: it featured observatories in high towers, underground laboratories designed to protect chemical experiments from the outside elements, and even a printing press, one of the first in Scandinavia. The one thing it didn't have, of course, was telescopes, as they weren't invented until the early seventeenth century. What's worse, they didn't even have long cardboard tubes that they could pretend to use as telescopes; cardboard wouldn't be invented until the *eighteenth* century.

Even without telescopes, Brahe's advanced instruments and dedication to scientific rigour were enough to turn astronomy into the first modern science, with a focus on data and evidence rather than just, you know, a *vibe*. Brahe's work added momentum to the growing Scientific Revolution that had kicked off with Nicolaus Copernicus publishing *De Revolutionibus Orbium Coelestium*, the first scientific work to properly lay out the dangerously heretical but ultimately correct idea that Earth orbits the sun, and not the other way around. This was a huge blow to narcissists everywhere, who on top of everything else now had to deal with the fact that all these bloody astronomers were *also* insisting that they weren't the centre of the universe.

Despite his astronomical expertise, Brahe never quite embraced the Copernican model of the solar system. Even if this landed him on the wrong side of the fence, scientifically speaking, it was a good career move, at the very least. Back then, endorsing the Copernican model would invariably result in many Christian churches cancelling you like you were a middle-aged stand-up comedian with half your routine dedicated to lamenting how you can't say anything these days and the other half dedicated to loudly going after politically marginalised people. Brahe avoided sixteenth-century cancel culture by proposing his own (thoroughly incorrect) model of the solar system, in which the *other* planets revolve around the sun, but not Earth. He was so close!

From a scientific standpoint, Brahe's legacy is extremely important. He catalogued the positions of the five known planets in the sky (Uranus and Neptune wouldn't be discovered until 1781 and 1846, respectively), enabling the prediction of their future movement. He also recorded the positions of stars with a greater level of accuracy than ever before, and helped to develop some of the most advanced astronomical equipment the world had ever seen.

From a non-scientific standpoint, Brahe's legacy is extremely wild, because when he wasn't making rigorous observations of the night sky, he was partying like it was 1599.[3] Brahe's royal stipend from King Frederick II was obscene—about 1 per cent of Denmark's governmental revenue—and he certainly didn't spend it all on science. Brahe used it to throw raging parties in Uraniborg, inviting rich and famous nobles from around Europe to come and have a piss-up with him on his island.

The stories that emerged from these parties are bizarre. Brahe loved a drink, and the shindigs he put on were raucous, debaucherous

3 Which, for a little while there, it was.

affairs as his guests raved and raged through the night. Like any noble worth their salt, Brahe kept a court jester—a man named Jepp—who was, by all accounts, one of the most entertaining blokes you'd ever meet and a favourite of Brahe's guests: Jepp was famed for not just his jests and japes but also his reported psychic abilities. Another character who made regular appearances at Brahe's rip-roarers was his pet elk,[4] who was, in a very literal sense, a party animal. This elk had a real taste for booze and would enthusiastically get on the grog, to the great amusement of Brahe's guests, routinely getting drunk as a skunk. Or, rather, getting loose as a moose.

Eventually, in 1596, Brahe fell from royal favour when Frederick II's successor, Christian IV, took power. Christian wasn't particularly interested in continuing to fund all of this expensive science, being much more interested in waging expensive wars instead. Consequently, Brahe was sent packing into exile. He moved to Prague, built an observatory and worked closely with his new assistant, a young fellow named Johannes Kepler, who would also go on to become an enormously important astronomer in his own right.[5]

---

4 The animal called an elk in Europe is exactly the same species as the animal called a moose in North America: *Alces alces*. This is distinct from the animal that Americans refer to as an elk, *Cervus canadensis*, a type of deer. Armed with your new-found knowledge of Cervidae, you're all but guaranteed to be the life of your next party.

5 And, interestingly enough, an extremely early author of science fiction. Aside from his work on boring scholastic pursuits—astronomy, mathematics, etc.—Kepler also found the time to write a novel, *Somnium*, in 1608. To give you an extremely brief summary, it tells the story of a 'daemon' who lives on the moon. It's considered one of the earliest examples of sci-fi; without Kepler, we may never have had *Star Wars*.

Sadly, however, their professional partnership was cut short in 1601, when Brahe attended a lavish feast. Brahe, who loved a banquet at the best of times, sat there and got stuck into the food and drink, and it wasn't long before he felt the need for a quick slash. However, to excuse himself from the banquet table would have been a serious breach of etiquette, so Brahe held it in. According to an account later written by Kepler, Brahe was so determined not to be rude that he remained in his seat, feeling like his back teeth were floating, eventually going from mild discomfort to excruciating agony. You might not have thought it medically possible to hold in your wee until your bladder bursts, but according to Kepler, this is what happened to Brahe: in refusing to be so ill-mannered as to excuse himself for a little trip to the privy, Brahe actually managed to rupture his bladder. His determination to be polite at all costs ended up giving an all-new meaning to the term 'dying for a wee'.

After the feast finally finished, Brahe hobbled home in intense pain. By this point he was unable to empty his bladder—he couldn't manage anything more than a few very painful drips and dribbles. The damage he had done to himself meant that it only got worse from there: he soon fell seriously ill, slipping in and out of delirium, and he died within two weeks of the feast, at the age of just 54.

Admittedly, the story of Brahe's death due to a ruptured bladder is based principally on Kepler's first-hand account of his master's refusal to leave the table to relieve himself and his seemingly consequent demise. Modern scientific investigations, however, offer slightly different explanations. Brahe's remains have been exhumed and examined, and while potential causes of death such as kidney stones or poisoning have been ruled out, Brahe's death may have had more to do with his general fondness for excess than his determination not to embarrass himself by getting up for a quick wee.

By the time he reached his 50s, all those years of wild partying had caught up with Brahe. He was badly overweight and had an unfortunate habit of binge-drinking, which hadn't left him in the best of nick. This means Brahe's death could have actually been caused by metabolic stress due to excessive alcohol consumption,[6] or perhaps as a result of untreated diabetes.[7]

Whatever caused Brahe's death, it was not a swift one, and not one that the poor astronomer was particularly proud of as a lasting legacy. The eleven agony-filled days he suffered through between the feast and his final moments were not pleasant for Brahe, but they did at least give him enough time to compose his own uncompromisingly honest epitaph: 'He lived like a sage and died like a fool.'

---

6 To be more specific, his lifelong love of booze might have landed him in a state of alcoholic ketoacidosis, which can be fatal. This long and rather crunchy medical term is understandably abbreviated to the acronym AKA, resulting in some medical texts introducing it as 'alcoholic ketoacidosis (aka AKA)'.

7 The fun with acronyms doesn't stop: complications with diabetes can result in someone entering into what's known as a hyperosmolar non-ketotic state. The life-threatening seriousness of this complication is somewhat undermined by the acronym used to refer to it: HONK.

24

Sir Arthur Aston

Beaten to Death with His Own Leg, 1649

A member of the minor English nobility in the seventeenth century, Sir Arthur Aston fought for King Charles I during the English Civil War. Charles didn't do a great job fighting this war—it's fair to say that he kind of lost his head over the whole affair, to be honest—but he wasn't the only one to suffer an untimely death. Aston, too, died in 1649, the very same year that Charles met his fate at the wrong end of a headsman's axe.

Aston was born in 1590, the son of another Sir Arthur Aston.[1] Arthur senior was a soldier, fighting for Catholic causes on the continent, and Arthur junior followed in his old man's footsteps once he was old enough to carry a sword. He fought across Poland, Sweden, and what is today Germany, rising through the ranks and becoming an experienced officer—wherever the righteous cause of Catholicism needed warm bodies holding sharp objects, Aston was there to fight against those godless, heretic Protestants. Except, after returning to England in the early 1640s, he fought *for* those godless, heretic Protestants, taking up the royalist cause of the Protestant King Charles I.

Aston wasn't a very popular figure among the royalists, who were also known as the Cavaliers: for one, he was a Catholic, which was just about the worst thing you could be in England at the time.[2] There wasn't a lot of common ground between the Cavaliers and their parliamentarian adversaries, the Roundheads, but no matter their opposing opinions on Charles, both sides were united in their strong dislike of those godless, heretic Catholics.

It wasn't just Aston's religious views that made him unpopular, however: it was also the fact that he was, by all accounts, just a little bit of a prick. He was a strict disciplinarian, and really didn't inspire much

---

1 It seems that baby name books really are a modern invention. Not only did we have all of those Matildas back in 1120, but now we have all of these Arthurs in the 1600s; over in France, they'd already had fourteen different kings called Louis, with a few more on the way.

2 Assuming you weren't Irish or, even worse, *French*.

affection from the troops under his command. All the same, there was no doubting he was a skilled and very experienced officer, and Charles needed all the help he could get in fighting the Roundheads, so Aston was sent off to fight as an officer in his army.

Sadly for Aston, in 1644 he lost a leg. Not in a glorious battle or anything like that: he just fell off a horse one day. This was a bugger of a thing for Aston—his injury was so severe that it required the amputation of his leg, and afterwards he hobbled about on a wooden prosthetic for the rest of his life. While this prosthetic helped him to retain a level of mobility, it would also be one of the reasons that the rest of Aston's life wasn't quite as long as he might have liked it to be.

Five years after this unfortunate incident, in 1649, Aston was stationed in Ireland. While this was during a pause in the English Civil War, there was still plenty of fighting to go around: Oliver Cromwell, the commander of the parliamentarian New Model Army, was also over in Ireland, fighting a war of conquest. Aston had been put in charge of Drogheda, an important coastal town in Ireland, and had orders to defend it from the rampaging Cromwell. Before long, however, along came Cromwell and his army, turning up with a view to seize control of Drogheda and its port as part of his ongoing takeover of Ireland.

After the parliamentarians besieged Drogheda, it didn't take too long for the town to fall. Unfortunately, Cromwell's men were none too gentle with the prisoners they took, which included Aston. These men were keen for loot and plunder; they craved the riches and booty that are so often the spoils of war. Such was the greed of these soldiers that, after capturing Aston, who was a minor noble and therefore a man of some evident wealth, they convinced themselves that Aston must have a hidden fortune somewhere. But where was it? They found neither hide nor hair of his supposed riches upon his person, but this did nothing to persuade these avaricious soldiers that it didn't exist.

So sure were they that Aston was holding out and refusing to hand over his gold, their eyes turned to his prosthetic leg. Aha, they thought, the perfect place to have safely ensconced your valuables; it *must* be filled with treasure! They hounded Aston, demanding that he show them how to open up this leg and access the trove he'd assuredly hidden inside.

Aston's protestations and denials fell on deaf ears. The soldiers then evidently decided that Aston's memory needed to be jogged—and what better to jog it with than with a leg?

They pulled off the prosthetic leg and then began to smack Aston about with it, pressing their demands that he hand over the treasure supposedly hidden within. He continued to protest, claiming that his leg was completely bereft of riches and was instead filled with, you know, *wood*, rather heavy wood that, he assured them based on ongoing firsthand experience, really did hurt quite a bit when put to use as a club.

These merciless soldiers, however, weren't taking no for an answer. They kept on beating Aston with his leg, not stopping until he was left a bruised and battered corpse. To add insult to injury,[3] when the

3 The injury, in this case, being Sir Arthur's.

soldiers finally broke open Aston's prosthetic leg, they found it completely bereft of any gold—proving once and for all that their claims of a treasure-filled prosthesis didn't have a leg to stand on.

25

François Vatel

Died Due to an Absence of Fish, 1671

In 1671, a chef named François Vatel died because a delivery of fish was late in arriving to a party. You probably want more details. Here they are.

Vatel was a very famous chef, who was known in particular for his masterful skill in making delicious pastries.[1] In time, Vatel's reputation as a master chef eventually saw him rise to become the

1 Vatel is also often incorrectly credited with the invention of Chantilly cream, which actually dates back around a century before his birth. It goes back to 1545, at the very least, appearing in an English cookbook entitled *A Proper Newe Booke of Cokerye*, as part of a recipe called *A Dyschefull of Snow*.

major-domo for Nicolas Fouquet, the Superintendent of Finances under the French king Louis XIV, known to history as the Sun King.

You might think that Fouquet would have been very pleased with himself to engage Vatel's services, but, believe it or not, hiring this famous chef ended up being Fouquet's undoing. In 1661, Vatel was put in charge of a great party: a sumptuous, lavish affair that served as a housewarming party (or chateau-warming, really, given it was being held in a grand, palatial residence) for the Superintendent of Finances.

Vatel did such a good job of putting on this party that King Louis XIV, who already didn't much like Fouquet, saw it as an excuse to lock up his superintendent before executing him. The grandness of the party gave Louis an excuse to accuse Fouquet of embezzling funds; he further charged him with deliberately embarrassing the office of king with the opulence of the celebration he'd organised.

This didn't prove too much of a setback for Vatel, however. Quite the opposite: it only *increased* his reputation, as he was now known to throw parties of such exceptional quality that even the Sun King himself was left in jealous awe! Vatel landed on his feet after Fouquet was locked up: he quickly got another job, this time as the major-domo of Louis II de Bourbon, Prince of Condé. He worked for the Grand Condé very successfully for ten years, this time managing to avoid getting his employer locked up by the king. Things were going very well for Vatel until 1671, the year he finally met his end.

In April, Vatel was commanded to arrange a royal banquet for 2,000 people in honour of Louis XIV, who would be visiting the Grand Condé's chateau. However, this banquet was being held at extremely short notice: Vatel had only two weeks to organise and prepare everything. A consummate professional, he immediately went about making preparations, determined to have this royal banquet live up to his highly exacting standards.[2] However, from the outset, more or less everything went wrong for him.

For instance, two days before the main event, there was a smaller preliminary feast, and there wasn't enough roast meat to go around to all of the tables. Vatel broke down, wept, and was sure his reputation and honour as a chef were forever destroyed. How could he bear the shame?

But it only got worse from there, as yet another disaster struck: that same evening, a thick fog settled over the chateau, ruining the fireworks display that Vatel had planned. Already beside himself after the catastrophe with the roast meat, Vatel started tearing out his hair, breaking down because of the disgrace and humiliation that this perfidious fog bank had caused him. The Grand Condé attempted to comfort the wretched Vatel, assuring him that everything was fine and that he should focus his attention on the preparations for the main banquet to make sure that it went off without a hitch.

As you can probably guess, though, it *still* only got worse from there.

The next day—the day before the royal banquet—Vatel was racing about, checking and double-checking everything to ensure that the event was going to be perfect. As he was running around

2 While still falling short, one hopes, of getting his employer executed.

like a headless chook, a delivery man arrived with two cartloads of seafood for the feast. Vatel was summoned to inspect the delivery, and he was horrified to discover that not enough fish had been brought.

'*C'est tout?*' Vatel asked the delivery man, aghast to think that this delivery was all that was coming to the chateau, and that he was going to have a repeat of the roast meat situation, but this time with fish.

'*Oui!*' answered the delivery man cheerfully. After all, that was all the fish he'd brought with him, and he didn't have any more with him to drop off.

What the delivery man didn't realise was that Vatel was actually asking if there were further deliveries coming *after this one*, which there indeed were—they were en route to the chateau at the time the first arrived. Vatel, rushed off his feet and thoroughly preoccupied, misunderstood and thought that this was the supplier confirming that there was *only* to be these two cartloads of fish and no more: nowhere near enough for a 2,000-person banquet!

This deficiency of seafood was unbearable for the already overwrought major-domo. First the roast meat, then the fireworks, and now the fish—it was too much. Mortified by the thought that there wouldn't be enough fish for everyone at the banquet that night, Vatel picked up a sword, ran to his bedroom and took his own life by impaling himself upon it.[3] Poor Vatel was so committed to his craft that he couldn't bear the thought of disgracing himself in front of his employer and the king, and would, quite literally, rather die.

---

3 Upon the sword, not the bedroom.

Which makes it all the more tragic to learn that his body was discovered by staff at the chateau a short time later, when they came to find Vatel and inform him that the rest of the fish had just arrived.

26

Jean-Baptiste 'Molière' Poquelin

Died of an Internal Haemorrhage in the Middle of a Stage Performance, 1673

You might have heard of Molière, the famous French actor, born as Jean-Baptiste Poquelin in 1622. Today, he's regarded as one of the finest French playwrights in history, famous in particular for his comedies. While both his life and his work were extremely influential on the development of the theatrical arts, his death—quite aside from being very strange—ended up influencing generations of superstitious actors, right through to the present day.

Molière was born into a well-heeled family and enjoyed a first-rate education before becoming an actor. This was seen as quite a significant step down, socially speaking—Molière's family was of a higher social class, and acting wasn't considered a particularly prestigious occupation back then. Unperturbed, Molière founded a theatre company at the age of 21, quickly went bankrupt and then—in the grand tradition of rich kids with rich parents everywhere—had his dad pay his debts so he could start again. Must be nice.

The second time around, things went better for the prodigal son. He began to use the stage name by which history remembers him—Molière[1]—and for the next decade or so he toured widely as part of a travelling theatre troupe. He didn't just perform: he also wrote his own plays, and some of his later plays would pass into legend. Works such as *Tartuffe*, *L'École des femmes*, and *Le Misanthrope* remain some of the most well-known and beloved pieces of French theatre, centuries after they were written.

In the 1660s, Molière's reputation as an actor and playwright captured the attention of Louis XIV, the Sun King himself.[2] With a royal patronage secured, Molière was off and away. He wrote and performed plays for the French upper classes, and while his preference and passion were for tragedies, it was instead his comedies, farces, and

1 Apparently he adopted a pseudonym in an attempt to allow his wealthy family to avoid the humiliation of being related to an actor.

2 The very same French king that poor François Vatel had been so worried about disappointing with a lack of fish.

satires that propelled him to fame and fortune, allowing him to enjoy a lot of success as a result.

Enjoying his success, though, didn't come easily to Molière. He ran himself ragged with his determination to improve—he always wanted to do more, and to do it better than ever—which ended up having a very negative impact on his health. He wasn't a particularly robust man as it was: the poor playwright had pulmonary tuberculosis, and working himself so hard did nothing to improve his condition. Despite taking breaks from acting here and there, his health steadily declined over time, and he ended up quite literally working himself to death.

In 1673, he put on what would be his final play, *Le Malade imaginaire*, which translates, funnily enough, as 'The Imaginary Invalid'. During his final performance on 17 February, Molière played the role of Argan, a hypochondriac. There was nothing imaginary about the malady he suffered halfway through the play, however: he collapsed, coughing up blood from an internal haemorrhage.

No matter! Molière was a showman through and through, and everyone in showbusiness knows that *the show must go on*. And go on it did! Molière was the opposite of a hypochondriac, it seems, as he managed to finish his performance to thunderous and, presumably, slightly worried applause. As soon as the play was over, however, Molière collapsed once again, and coughed up even more blood from an even bigger haemorrhage. The tuberculosis he had been carrying around for years had finally presented its bill—one that Molière couldn't afford to pay—and so he died very shortly thereafter.

Socially speaking, actors at this time were considered to have a very low standing. Indeed, French law actually forbade actors from being buried in consecrated ground. Molière's friends couldn't find a priest who was willing to attend to him before he died so he could renounce the evils of treading the boards and receive the last rites; consequently, Molière had to be buried in a section of a cemetery that was otherwise reserved for unbaptised infants. Today, however, after having been reinterred, he can be found in Père Lachaise Cemetery, Paris, alongside other French artistic luminaries such as Édith Piaf, Marcel Proust, and Frédéric Chopin.[3]

And that was the end of the most famous French playwright of all time: Molière's dedication to the stage became his undoing. Nonetheless, in theatres all around the world today, his lasting legacy is still felt. Even in theatres that have never staged his plays, superstitious actors know to avoid the colour green because of how unlucky it is for those in their profession. The reason behind this is, believe it or not, the death of Molière—as he lay there coughing up blood halfway through his last performance, he was clothed all in green.

3 Who was, of course, also proudly Polish, as the airport in Warsaw is so determined to remind us.

27

Bhai Mati Das, Bhai Sati Das, Bhai Dayala, and Guru Tegh Bahadur

Executed in Inventively Horrific Ways, 1675

In 1675, four Sikhs—a guru and three of his followers—were all executed on the orders of Mughal emperor Aurangzeb, who managed to come up with some wonderfully grisly ways to do away with these religious dissidents. When it came to executions, Aurangzeb certainly wasn't in the business of efficiency, as he didn't just line up his poor Sikh prisoners and hang 'em, oh no. Instead, they died in ways that really cast the phrase 'cruel and unusual punishment' in a new light.

The Sikh religion was founded in the late fifteenth century, and during the following years several gurus—spiritual leaders—were instrumental in developing the religion as it grew and gained new followers. Throughout its history, however, Sikhism has faced its fair share of challenges—such as in the 1670s, when the Mughal Empire got stuck into some pretty full-on persecution of not just Sikhs but also non-Muslims in general.

Despite having increased the territory of the Mughal Empire to its largest extent, ridding his imperial government of corruption, and his generous patronage of art and culture, Aurangzeb left a historical legacy heavily marred by his immense religious intolerance. His oppressive religious policies saw strict taxes levied on non-Muslims, Hindu and Sikh temples and other non-Muslim places of worship desecrated and destroyed, and the persecution and murder of those who refused to accept Islam.

And it was this persecution that saw the ninth Sikh guru, Guru Tegh Bahadur, captured and executed along with three of his most devoted followers: two brothers, named Bhai Mati Das and Bhai Sati Das, and a third man named Bhai Dayala. Tegh Bahadur had been named guru in 1664, and since then had travelled the Indian subcontinent, not just preaching Sikhism but also encouraging resistance to the religious oppression of the Mughals. He didn't limit himself to protecting Sikhs, but also also lent aid and support to persecuted Hindus.

This ongoing resistance ultimately led to the arrest of Guru Tegh Bahadur in 1675, whereby Emperor Aurangzeb made his displeasure with him and his followers very clear indeed. They had been causing problems for him all over the place while he was simply trying to get on with the business of good old-fashioned religious persecution; they had made an enormous nuisance of themselves by protecting Sikhs and Hindus from the Mughal authorities instead of gratefully accepting the jackboot of faith-based oppression. Now, they would pay the price.

Following the arrest of Tegh Bahadur and his three devotees, they were brought to the city of Delhi in November 1675. There, the emperor made a simple request of the guru: to prove his religion was the true one, rather than Islam, by performing a miracle for all to see. If he couldn't, then he had a straightforward choice: to convert to Islam, or to be executed.

As a red-blooded Sikh, firm in his convictions,[1] Guru Tegh Bahadur chose death. This death wasn't given to him easily, though: Aurangzeb was actually reluctant to execute the guru, knowing that martyring Tegh Bahadur would only strengthen the convictions of many of his followers. As a result, in order to give the guru more of an incentive to embrace Islam, Aurangzeb announced that if Tegh Bahadur wouldn't convert, his three disciples would be tortured and put to death in horrific ways.

---

1 And completely unable to perform the requested miracle, for what it's worth.

These terms were evidently acceptable to the steadfast guru. He and the three others were taken to a public square, where, in front of the huge crowd that had eagerly assembled to see the action, Tegh Bahadur's three followers were killed in some of the most nightmarish ways imaginable.

The first to die, Bhai Mati Das, was tied securely between two upright posts so he couldn't move. The Mughals then produced a huge two-man crosscut saw, the kind you'd use to fell a giant tree with a lumberjack at each end. Facing the guru, and with both in a state of seemingly perfect calm, Bhai Mati Das was then sawn in half. However—and here's where it really starts to get nasty—this wasn't done in the style of a magician sawing an assistant in a box in half, across the waist. Instead, the luckless Bhai Mati Das was sawn in half *vertically*, from his head to his groin, completely bifurcated right down the middle. At least they started with his head. Imagine if they'd started from his . . . actually, no, *don't* imagine that.

Bhai Mati Das may have gone to pieces, but Tegh Bahadur didn't. He continued his firm refusal to convert, and so Bhai Dayala was up next. Lucky him.

Bhai Dayala was tied up with big chains, in a way you might see in a cartoon: it was as though he was in an oversized cocoon. Once tied up like this, he was then put into a massive cauldron that had been filled with water, as the Mughals went about preparing the *soup du jour*: cream of Bhai Dayala, seasoned with artisanal, hand-wrapped iron chains.

A fire was lit under the cauldron, and the unfortunate Bhai Dayala was slowly boiled alive. Once again, though, there wasn't a flicker on the unwavering Tegh Bahadur's face, even after Bhai Dayala's body was taken out of the cauldron and roasted in a fire until it was nothing but blackened charcoal.

Only Bhai Sati Das remained. He was taken by the Mughals and wrapped up in cotton wool, which—as he'd just watched his brother and their friend get sawn in half and boiled—presumably made Bhai Sati Das feel as though he was being dealt with exceptionally leniently. Cotton wool is certainly preferable to chains, anyway, right?

Well, no, because chains don't *burn*. Bhai Sati Das and his cotton wool were soaked in oil and set alight, and Tegh Bahadur once again watched, impassive, as his third devotee died in a torturously hideous fashion. Chopped up, boiled, and now set on fire—Aurangzeb had some very diverse and inventive methods of execution! The assembled crowd certainly got their money's worth: it was like a little variety show for them. No one wants to see the same trick twice.

With Bhai Mati Das, Bhai Dayala, and Bhai Sati Das all dead, and with Tegh Bahadur still unswerving and resolute on the question of his conversion to Islam, his time had finally come; his open defiance of Emperor Aurangzeb would finally be punished. And given that his followers had all suffered such horrible, agonising deaths, Aurangzeb must have been saving up something *really* special for the Sikh leader.

The Mughals took Tegh Bahadur and made him sit in front of an executioner who held a wickedly sharp sword. You won't believe what happened next: the executioner raised his sword and . . . chopped off Tegh Bahadur's head.

Yeah. A bit of a letdown: just a run-of-the-mill beheading, been done a thousand times, nothing special about it. Certainly not the spectacular finale you may have been expecting after the excitingly innovative deaths that had preceded it.

Perhaps Aurangzeb was out of ideas by then, or maybe he just wanted it over and done with. After all, there's no point dragging it out. The guru made it abundantly clear that he wasn't going to convert, so why not just lop off his head so we can all go home? Perhaps we should be *glad* that Tegh Bahadur got a quick and clean death, unlike his followers.

In any case, these three horrific and one routine executions did, ultimately, martyr these four Sikhs for their religion. Right through to the modern era, on 24 November each year, Sikhs around the world still observe Guru Tegh Bahadur's *Shaheedi Divas*, his day of martyrdom, and commemorate the lives of the guru and his followers. Or, rather, their deaths.

28

Jean-Baptiste Lully

Died after Hitting His Foot with a Stick while Performing, 1687

After that brief trip to the subcontinent, we return now to seventeenth-century Paris and its performing arts scene, to talk about the death of another famous French artist, who throughout much of his career was actually a colleague of poor Molière: the composer and musician Jean-Baptiste Lully. Not only did these two share the same given names, but Lully *also* died due to his unflinching dedication to performance.

Born in Italy in 1632, Lully moved to France around 1646, at the age of just fourteen. He had an obvious talent for music and performance, playing the violin and guitar, singing beautifully, and also dancing like a seventeenth-century Channing Tatum.

Lully's talents ended up catching the eye of the young King Louis XIV, who seems to be a recurring character in this book.[1] After this, Lully rose through the royal court and did very well for himself under Louis's patronage, writing all sorts of music from dances and marches to ballets and operas, demonstrating immense artistic inventiveness and innovation. Today, even if Lully isn't as famous as other baroque-period composers such as Bach and Vivaldi, his music is still absolutely exquisite and among the best to emerge from the period; go and listen to his *Marche pour la cérémonie des Turcs* if you need convincing.

In his own time, Lully was very famous for his many operas, as well as for being a talented dancer. He loved to put on a show: his ballets, in particular, were true spectacles, and people flocked to see them performed in all their lavish glory.

Eventually, and rather sadly, he lost the favour of Louis XIV, when it emerged that Lully may have enjoyed the intimate company of both ladies *and* gentlemen. This was something to which the French king took an unfortunately dim view, and so Lully was in the royal bad books from then on. Not to be put off, though, the tenacious Lully sought to regain the king's favour by putting on a special performance of his famous work *Te Deum* to celebrate the king recovering from

---

1 Despite his regular appearances in these pages, Louis XIV doesn't get his own chapter because his death wasn't all that strange: he died of gangrene at the age of 76.

some surgery. Unfortunately, this decision, coupled with Lully's great love of dancing, ended up being the death of him.

Lully oversaw a spirited performance of *Te Deum* for the king's pleasure, conducting the orchestra with passion and fervour. However, rather than the delicate little white baton you might associate with orchestral conductors these days, he used a big, heavy stick. And while conducting with this staff by banging it on the floor to keep time, Lully accidentally brought it down on his own foot, hitting it so hard that he injured himself quite badly.

After the performance, the wound became so badly infected that gangrene set in, meaning the leg needed to be amputated if Lully were to survive. Gangrenous necrosis—usually referred to simply as gangrene—takes place when bodily tissue fails to receive enough blood to survive, and this will cause the affected area to swell painfully, turning red and then black as the tissue dies. It usually affects the extremities—the hands and feet—and when left untreated can be deadly, even today. Antibiotics can halt the spread of gangrene, while dead tissue must be surgically removed to prevent the continued spread of infection. Fail to treat gangrene, and it will often be fatal.

When doctors told Lully that he had to choose between losing his leg or his life, it was hardly the news he wanted to hear. Lully loved to dance more than just about anything, and the loss of a leg would mean the end of his dancing career. That prospect was enough for Lully to completely refuse to let the doctors cut off his leg: the only thing he wanted to cut was a rug. He simply couldn't bear the thought of spending the rest of his life unable to dance.

And it might be accurate to say that Lully got his wish because, technically speaking, he was able to dance on that leg until the day he died[2]—a day that came along not long after the gangrene set in. After his self-inflicted foot wound became gangrenous, dead tissue spread up his leg, which he still steadfastly refused to let the doctors amputate. Consequently, Lully died three months after this onstage incident with the staff, and he went down in history as one of *two* seventeenth-century French artists to die because of their uncompromising dedication to authentic performance.

2 Albeit extremely painfully.

29

Hannah Twynnoy

The First Person in Britain to Be Killed by a Tiger, 1703

We don't know who the first person killed by a tiger was. It would have been a long time ago: tigers have existed for over two million years, well and truly making us newcomers as far as they're concerned. *Homo sapiens* like you and me have only been around for roughly 300,000 years, so perhaps the first person to die in a tiger attack was the victim of an inquisitive tiger investigating what was going on with this brand-new, tasty-looking, hairless ape precariously tottering along on two legs. If that were the case, it would seem that the old saying about curiosity killing the cat was about as wrong as it could possibly be: instead, curiosity killed the proto-human, and left the cat with a nice full belly.

Even if we don't know who the first person to be killed by a tiger was, we do know who the first person killed by a tiger *in Britain* was, which is a very unusual and unfortunate historical distinction to have. Tigers, generally speaking, have no business being in Britain. They're not suited to life there: most tigers prefer warmer climates, they're not known for their ability to line up in orderly queues, they're not huge on drinking tea, and they tend to have excellent teeth.

No, Britain isn't the place for a tiger. Nor is it, while we're on big cats, the place for a lion, but that hasn't stopped the British adopting the lion as their national animal. Ordinarily, a country will tend to pick a national animal that actually lives within the country itself, but not the British—despite the British Isles not being a natural habitat for the lion, it remains in pride of place as one of their national emblems. They're not alone in this regard, either. The lion is the national animal of many European nations, including the Netherlands, Belgium, the Czech Republic, and North Macedonia—although, in fairness, lion fossils have been uncovered all across Europe, dating back hundreds of thousands of years, and lions may have lived in Britain as few as 12,000 years ago. Perhaps British heraldists just have very, very long memories.[1]

In any case, *tigers* have never lived in Britain—historically, they never got further west than eastern Turkey—and so the unfortunate

1 Not that Australians should be lecturing anyone on national animals and heraldry: Australia is one of the few nations on Earth that very enthusiastically *eats* its own national animals.

tiger-induced death of Hannah Twynnoy in 1703 was a very unusual and unlikely one indeed. Twynnoy was born around 1670, and worked as a barmaid at a pub called the White Lion Inn[2] located in the small English town of Malmesbury. We know very little else about her life or her family, as the strange nature of her death is the only thing that caused the history books to find space for her in the first place. Understandably so, as it's not all that often that someone gets killed by a tiger in a little English town like Malmesbury.

The pressing question is, of course, what was a tiger doing in a little English town like Malmesbury in the first place? Local history tells us of a visiting circus; however, this isn't quite accurate: travelling circuses as we know them today didn't exist in 1703. The first performing act that could be characterised as a modern circus (as opposed to the ancient circus that kept Romans entertained with chariot races and the like) dates back to the equestrian shows put on from 1768 onwards by a former cavalry officer, Philip Astley, who would bring out acrobats and clowns to entertain the audience between the equestrian acts. Travelling menageries, however, certainly did exist, and one seems to have come to Malmesbury in 1703, bringing a tiger along with it. Further, the people involved with this travelling menagerie likely lodged at the White Lion Inn, meaning that as someone who worked there, Twynnoy would have been in close proximity to the

---

2 More references to big cats, overlooking all the poor wildlife native to the British Isles. Why not the White Badger Inn, or the White Pine Marten Inn? If you want to name your pub after a large mammal that is *actually* British, why not the White Red Deer Inn?

strange and exotic creatures that were visiting the town—including the tiger that is said to have brought about her end.

The story of Twynnoy's death drifts between history and legend, and it's difficult to conclusively say how much of it is true. Many sources agree, however, that Twynnoy may have played a rather injudicious role in bringing about her own demise, as a passage from John Moffatt's 1805 book *The History of the Town of Malmesbury*[3] indicates:

> Hannah Twynnoy . . . was a servant of the White Lion Inn, where there was an exhibition of wild beasts, and among the rest a very fierce tiger, which she imprudently took a pleasure in teasing, notwithstanding the repeated remonstrances of its keeper. One day, whilst amusing herself with this dangerous diversion, the enraged animal, by an extraordinary effort, drew out the staple,[4] sprang towards the unhappy girl, caught hold of her gown, and tore her to pieces.

---

3 The full title of Moffatt's book is actually *The History of the Town of Malmesbury, and of Its Ancient Abbey, the Remains of which Magnificent Edifice are still used as a Parish Church; together with Memoirs of Eminent Natives and other Distinguished Characters who were Connected with the Abbey or Town, to which is Added, an Appendix (Embellished with Engravings).* Efforts to give the book you read now a similarly resplendent title ended, most regrettably, in failure.

4 'Staple', here, is an old term for the fastening mechanism on the tiger's enclosure, not a tiny strip of metal used to hold paper together. Even if they'd had access to staples as we know them today back in 1703, it's unlikely they would have used them to keep a tiger locked up.

The overwhelming majority of people are forgotten by history; few forge themselves a legacy worthy of inclusion in the history books. Hannah Twynnoy, however, secured her place in the annals of time not just by rather foolishly taunting a tiger until it mauled her to death but also by doing so in a country where a tiger had no business being in the first place. Had this happened in India, or Indonesia, or another region where tigers are more commonplace, historians wouldn't have bothered to lift a pen. But as she was the first person to be killed by a tiger in Britain, Twynnoy's unique death was specifically noted in local death records: 'Hannah Twynney Kild by a Tygre at ye White Lyon.' Centuries later, her highly unusual death continues to be commemorated—you can visit the town of Malmesbury and find her tombstone, which to this day has a remarkably poetic epitaph etched upon it:

> In bloom of Life
> She's snatchd from hence,
> She had not room
> To make defence;
> For Tyger fierce
> Took Life away.
> And here she lies
> In a bed of Clay,
> Until the Resurrection Day.

30

King Adolf Frederick of Sweden

Died after Having a Little Bit Too Much Dessert, 1771

For the two decades between 1751 and 1771, the Kingdom of Sweden was ruled by King Adolf Frederick of the House of Holstein-Gottorp. Born in 1710, Adolf Frederick was installed as king at 40 years of age, after having been the Prince-Bishop of Lübeck since 1727. The previous Swedish king, Frederick I, died without any legitimate heirs, and so mild-mannered Adolf Frederick was elected to succeed him, despite not being a direct relation.[1] This took place in a period of Swedish history when their kings didn't have a lot of power. Instead, the parliamentary *Riksens Ständer*—Riksdag of the Estates—held most of the power throughout the kingdom, and kings such as Adolf Frederick were little more than figureheads. Real political decision-making was done by the Riksdag, whenever its competing factions could find the time; rather than focus on the important business of governing the realm, these factions were often far too busy focusing on the even more important business of fighting among themselves.

These parliamentary factions, incidentally, were called the Hats (*Hattarna*) and the Caps (*Mössorna*), both named after pieces of headwear. The Hats were a conservative nationalist party that gained their nickname due to their famous association with the tricorne hat worn by military officers. The Caps, on the other hand, gained their nickname initially as an insult: they were known derisively as the 'nightcaps' because of their military timidity and liberalist views. Even so, the Caps embraced their nickname despite the malice behind it, perhaps purely out of respect for the historical neatness of having both parties named after pieces of headwear. This sort of thing really should be brought back. Instead of the boring names that political parties tend to have these days—such as 'the Conservative Party' or 'the Greens'—imagine heading to the ballot box to vote for the Pearl Necklace Party or the Birkenstock Brigade.

1 Then again, this is European royalty we're talking about, for whom the strict definition of a 'direct relation' has been buried under centuries of them marrying their own cousins.

In any case, Adolf Frederick took the Swedish throne and happily got on with the business of doing very little as a figurehead monarch. He did make an attempt or two to reassert absolutist rule, but this was quickly shut down by the Riksdag. Even if the Hats and the Caps hated each other, there's one thing they hated more: the idea of absolute monarchy returning to Sweden.

Overall, Sweden did alright for itself during this period. The kingdom enjoyed a time of relative peace, as well as experiencing several important progressive reforms once the Caps took power. For instance, the 1766 *Freedom of the Press Act* was ahead of its time in giving . . . well, a lot of freedom to the press; unsurprisingly, it was exactly what it said on the tin. This Act was a remarkably forward-thinking piece of legislation: a broadly uncensored press is something we take for granted today, but it was very unusual for the time.

As for Adolf Frederick personally, even if he was weak-willed and about as effective in politics as a screen door on a submarine, he was by all accounts a rather nice fellow. He was a dutiful husband and an affectionate father, he was very kind to his staff and servants, and he greatly enjoyed a personal hobby: making, of all things, ornate little snuff boxes.

The other thing he greatly enjoyed, however, was his food—so much so that it may have been the end of him.

Shrove Tuesday is the last day before the Christian festival of Lent, which traditionally involves a 40-day period of fasting or giving up your favourite food or drink. Consequently, Shrove Tuesday is the last chance for a devoted Christian to properly enjoy stuffing their face for a good while. Adolf Frederick was indeed a devoted Christian, and, as we've established, he also loved his tucker. He wasn't about to pass up the opportunity for one last[2] top-notch feed when Shrove Tuesday came around.

On 12 February 1771—Shrove Tuesday—Adolf Frederick organised a splendid feast: one that was, quite literally, fit for a king. At this feast, he got on the lobster and the caviar, he knocked back the champagne—Adolf Frederick was enthusiastically eating and drinking like there was no tomorrow. Which, for him, there wouldn't be.

Soon enough, dessert was served, and it was his very favourite: *hetvägg*, little sweet rolls (*semlor*) served with cream and hot milk. Adolf Frederick was unable to contain himself, perhaps dreading the thought of giving up all this for Lent, and so went a little bit mental. The king helped himself to no fewer than fourteen servings of *hetvägg*, and, unsurprisingly, immediately began to experience a fair bit of digestive distress. Adolf Frederick's condition worsened as time passed, and after an evening of biting into *semlor*, the next thing he bit was the dust.

It remains unconfirmed that it was the fourteen servings of *hetvägg*—on top of all the lobster and caviar and champagne—that actually killed the king, but no matter how you look at it, his gluttony certainly didn't help. Adolf Frederick was known to be in poor health already, and the royal autopsy tactfully drew no connection between

---

2 In this specific case, that 'last' was rather more literal than Adolf Frederick may have expected.

the king's excessive eating and his subsequent death that very same night. Official records instead tell us that Adolf Frederick died of a stroke—but while correlation doesn't imply causation,[3] you'd think that stuffing himself silly on *semlor* might have played some kind of a role in his premature demise.

When you eat too much, a number of things happen to your body. Your stomach expands beyond its normal size to accommodate all the food you're chucking down into it, causing a feeling of discomfort as it pushes against surrounding internal organs. An over-full stomach can also cause the hydrochloric acid within it to be forced up the oesophagus—this is known as acid reflux, and it's what causes the very unpleasant sensation of heartburn. Overeating doesn't just affect the stomach, however: your entire body responds, with your liver and pancreas creating extra hormones and enzymes to help handle all this extra food, and a feeling of sluggishness may overtake you as the body's resources are sent to the intestines to speed up your digestive system.

And it's not only the digestive system that accelerates. After a huge meal, your entire metabolism has to kick into gear, as your body works overtime to process all the food you've just put into it. This is why you might feel hot or sweaty after eating a lot: it's your body working very hard to burn through a tonne of extra kilojoules as quickly as it can. And powering this elevated metabolic response is

3 A concept very handily illustrated by the example that ice-cream sales and sunburn rates rise and fall in correlation to one another. It's not that ice-cream causes sunburn; it's just that you're more likely to both eat ice-cream and spend time out in the sun on a hot summer's day.

your heart, which has to beat faster and harder in order to help your metabolism to speed up.

This is hardly the sort of thing you hope for as an unwell 60-year-old with existing stomach problems thanks to a history of overeating, which is exactly what King Adolf Frederick of Sweden was. The stately, official documentation regarding Adolf Frederick's death employs discreetly euphemistic language—'His Majesty died about three hours after his dinner, which consisted of strong and rich food'—but there's no escaping that there must have been some sort of link between an old man with digestive issues putting away fourteen helpings of dessert and then not living to see the next morning.

King Adolf Frederick's love of food meant that he literally ate himself to death—perhaps not in the short term, but *definitely* in the long term—proving that you really can have too much of a good thing.[4] Then again, it wasn't all bad: at least he didn't have to give up anything for Lent that year.

4 As one online commenter noted, if Adolf Frederick died after eating fourteen *semlor*, the limit is evidently thirteen.

31

Lewis Fenton and Sir William Payne Gallwey

Killed by Turnips, 1833 and 1881

If you had a dollar for every time a member of the British Parliament had suffered a turnip-related death, you'd have two dollars. Which isn't a lot, but it's strange that it's happened twice.

Captain Lewis Fenton, born in 1780, was a British military officer who had fought for king and country as a red-blooded Englishman, serving as a captain in the 55th Regiment of Foot. Between 1800 and 1820, his regiment was deployed all around the world, to places such as the Netherlands, South Africa, and the West Indies, so Fenton was likely very well-travelled indeed by the time he retired from military service.

It seems that once he moved on from his time as a soldier, Fenton led a more sedate life. He settled down in Huddersfield, in northern England, and was elected to parliament as a Whig[1] MP. From all appearances, Fenton enjoyed the peace and quiet of his later years, and took great pleasure in a rather more pastoral lifestyle. Outside his country home, he kept cattle and grew vegetables, which sounds truly idyllic after all that time as a soldier.

And you would think that, having retired from the military, the most dangerous part of his life was behind him. After all, being a career soldier *has* to be more dangerous than living in a nice country manor and growing turnips, doesn't it?

Not in Captain Fenton's case, it seems, as this tragic article from the *Preston Chronicle* in 1833 tells us:

> On Wednesday (Nov. 27) the town of Huddersfield was thrown into the greatest consternation, in consequence of a report that Capt. Fenton, M.P. for that borough, had fallen out of an upper

---

1 The Whigs were a liberal political party in Britain that opposed the conservative Tories, and they were just one letter away from following in the Swedish tradition of being named after headwear. The true etymology of the term Whig, however, is completely out of left field: it comes from the truncation of the word 'whiggamore', a disdainful nickname given to Scottish cattle drovers.

window in his house, and been so dreadfully injured as not to be likely to recover. The excitement was much increased by vague rumours being circulated as to the cause of the lamented gentleman's melancholy death.

Mary Stead, the housemaid of Capt. Fenton, said . . . she went upstairs into the garret,[2] and found it in the same state as usual; but the window, which opened at the top, was wide open. There was a little chair under the window, which was always placed there . . . He often went into the garret, to see if the cows were right.

Mr. William Wilks, surgeon, of Huddersfield . . . examined him, and found a wound about three inches in length on the prominent part of the forehead, just above the right eye. On further examination he found an extensive fracture of the skull. A portion of the brain protruded, which he removed.

[Fenton] could speak, and [Wilks] asked him some questions, which he answered in a very incoherent manner . . . on his asking him how he was, he shook hands with him most cordially. [Wilks] knew of nothing which could cause excitement; when he last saw [the] deceased he was in excellent spirits.

Mr. Wilks . . . mentioned some conversation which he had had with Mrs. Fenton, in which she had stated that her husband was in the habit of going into the garret, (whence it was supposed that he had fallen,) for the purpose of looking out of the window into a piece

2 An old term for an attic. The etymology of the term 'garret' is much less interesting than that of 'Whig'—it comes from the Old French word *garir*, 'to defend', which also gives us the modern English word 'garrison'.

> of ground where some turnips were growing, to see that none of his cows were trespassing in it.

The hapless Fenton paid the ultimate price for his vigilance in making sure that the cows weren't getting into his turnips: he fell out of his upstairs window into the turnip patch itself and died shortly thereafter. Even when facing down death, however, the gentlemanly Fenton's manners didn't fail him—he gave the good doctor Wilks a firm handshake on his way out. After a long career as a soldier, the thing that brought him undone was instead the simple—and generally non-lethal—turnip.

And that, you'd be forgiven for thinking, *must* be the only example of a British MP coming to an untimely end because of turnips.

On the contrary!

Sir William Payne Gallwey, the Tory member for Thirsk, proudly served his constituency for almost three decades, between 1851 and 1880. He retired that year, as he was in his seventies, and gave his life over to more recreational pursuits that befitted a country gentleman. For instance, he'd go out shooting, a beloved pastime of the landed gentry. After all, someone's got to teach those blasted pheasants a lesson; someone's got to put all those loathsome ducks in their place!

However, his career as a hunter was cut short one day in 1881, when a most unfortunate accident took place while he was out hunting. Uh oh, you're thinking, what manner of fearsome beast did he encounter? Was he torn to pieces by a wild animal? Did a particularly aggressive goose savagely maul him to death?

Well, no. According to a news report in the *Northern Echo*, while Gallwey 'was out shooting in the parish of Bagby . . . in crossing a turnip field fell with his body on to a turnip, sustaining severe internal injuries'.

In other words, Gallwey tripped over and landed on a turnip, which busted him up so badly that he died. Even being armed with a shotgun didn't help him. So much for all the people who say that a good guy with a gun is the only way to stop a bad turnip without a gun.

In fairness, Gallwey was well into his seventies, so he wasn't exactly in peak physical condition; nevertheless, 'killed by a turnip' isn't exactly what you want for an epitaph, is it? With some selective reporting, his death can be dressed up to sound a little more impressive: the technically true 'he died in a hunting accident' conjures up the idea that he was attacked by a bear, or was eaten by a tiger, or came to some other gloriously violent demise. Just don't give people the details: he died in a hunting accident, enough said. We will exercise our discretion, and not go on to mention that he was slain not by a ferocious beast of the hunt, but by a humble root vegetable.

32

Archduchess Mathilda of Austria

Killed by Her Smoking Habit (But in a New and Exciting Way), 1867

On 25 January 1849, Archduchess Mathilda Marie Adelgunde Alexandra of Austria was born to Hildegard Luise Charlotte Theresia Friederike von Bayern and her husband Archduke Albrecht Friedrich Rudolf Dominik, Duke of Teschen. Austrian birth certificates must have had a fair bit of room on them back then.

Through her dad, Archduchess Mathilda was a descendant of former Holy Roman Emperor Leopold II, while on her mum's side, her grandfather was King Ludwig I of Bavaria. Suffice to say, young Mathilda had some *extremely* blue blood in her veins. As a result, Archduke Albrecht had big plans for his daughter. He organised a marriage between her and an Italian prince, Umberto,[1] the heir apparent to the Italian throne. This would make Mathilda the Queen Consort of Italy, a fitting position for one of her pedigree. But as you may have guessed, the marriage between Mathilda and Umberto never came about, and for good reason: the unlucky archduchess died at the age of just eighteen, in circumstances that are both tragic and—it has to be said—pretty funny.

Smoking kills. We all know that now. Harmful chemicals found in every lungful of cigarette smoke include formaldehyde (used in preserving dead tissue), ammonia (used in commercial cleaning products), and hydrogen cyanide (used in illegal chemical warfare). The nicotine in cigarettes is not only extremely addictive, but also damages your cardiovascular system; the tar in cigarettes coats the insides of your lungs like soot in a chimney.

Whether it's with emphysema, lung cancer, heart disease, or any number of other deadly ailments, cigarettes will kill you, one way or another. This wasn't always as abundantly obvious as it is now: in the first half of the 20th century, doctors actually prescribed cigarettes as therapeutic, with some actively promoting them in advertising. As late as the 1950s, it was common to see ads featuring smiling doctors

1 Do yourself a favour and have a look at pictures of Umberto I of Italy: he had the most *absurd* moustache you'll ever see. The thing is massive. It looks like a bad Photoshop job, or a video game cosmetic that was incorrectly scaled.

holding cigarettes, with slogans like 'Just What the Doctor Ordered', '84% of English Doctors Prefer a Mild Cigarette', and the very confusing 'More Doctors Smoke Camels'.

Thankfully, and in spite of the persistent lies of Big Tobacco and their bottomless pits of advertising and lobbying money, these days it seems that basic medical and scientific truth has prevailed. Most of the world now recognises that smoking is a bad habit that will—eventually—bring you to an untimely and unpleasant end.

The difficult part in convincing people of this, however, has always been a lack of immediacy. After all, it's not like you light up a dart and that's that, you keel over dead. Rather, it takes time: it can take years and years for a smoker to develop the horrific and debilitating illnesses that smoking causes.

As a result of this time frame, it's very difficult to get the message across to a teenager that munching on durries will kill them. All that cancer stuff is *decades* away, and to an adolescent a decade might as well be a *thousand* years, not ten. Who cares about lung cancer, they say—let's go down behind the cricket nets after school and get on the Winnie Blues![2]

However, in the case of one specific teenager, Archduchess Mathilda of Austria, her smoking habit *did* kill her with a startling—and tragic—level of immediacy.

On 6 June 1867, Mathilda put on her glad rags and got ready to head out for a night in town. Wearing a lovely gauze dress, she talked

2 Or, with the advent of plain cigarette packaging, the Winnie Drab Dark Brown (Pantone 448 C)s.

with her cousin Friedrich about their plans to go to the theatre that evening. At one point, she moved over to a window to light up a sneaky cigarette and start smoking. While she was standing at the window, however, she heard her dad approaching the room with other members of her family.

Archduke Albrecht was said to be very old-fashioned when it came to political affairs and his job as the Inspector-General of the Austro-Hungarian Army. Indeed, many historians consider Austria's broad failure in the First World War to be due in some part to the fact that the archduke failed to modernise the Austrian military in the later stages of the nineteenth century—he just didn't keep up with the times. Be that as it may, Archduke Albrecht certainly was well *ahead* of the times when it came to smoking, as he had strictly forbidden his kids from choofing on the ciggies.

Thus, due to her father's intense disapproval of smoking, when Mathilda heard him coming, she swiftly hid her lit cigarette behind her back because she didn't want to get in trouble with her old man. Luckily, she was quick enough to avoid her dad noticing the cigarette, and because she was near the window, the smell of the smoke wasn't obvious. Close one!

Albrecht and the rest of her family hung around in the room with Mathilda, chatting away pleasantly. Suddenly, Mathilda burst into flames.

From their perspective, it honestly looked like she had spontaneously combusted, and the poor girl went up in flames so quickly and was burned so badly that she died.

At first, her family members were at a complete loss. They were devastated, of course, but also entirely unable to explain what had actually happened. How had Mathilda simply burst into flames like that, before their very eyes? This remained a tragic mystery until cousin Friedrich dobbed in Mathilda to Albrecht. Friedrich revealed that Mathilda was secretly a smoker, and that the cigarette she'd hidden must have set her highly flammable gauze dress alight.

So, young readers everywhere: listen to your parents when they tell you that smoking kills, because they're right[3]—in more ways than one!

But if you're going to ignore your parents' sage advice and still try to sneakily smoke without them noticing, don't wear highly flammable clothing when you do: be sensible, and wear clothing made out of inflammable material, such as asbestos.

3 Unfortunately, parents usually end up being right about most things. It's truly infuriating.

33

Mary Ward

Killed in a Car Accident Before Cars Were Even a Thing, 1869

These days, well over a million people are killed worldwide on the roads every year. Cars are very dangerous things, and unfortunately people seem all too ready to forget that. Then again, with about a billion and a half vehicles driving on the world's roads, it's unsurprising that there are going to be accidents and deaths, as there are just too many cars on the roads today for us to avoid them.

This thought only makes the death of Mary Ward all the more tragic, because when she was killed by a car in 1869, there weren't really *any* cars on the roads; she was the first person in history known to die in this way.

Ward, who was born in 1827 as Mary King, was an Irish scientist—and a good one, too.[1] She was into all sorts of stuff, but principally optics, astronomy, and entomology. When her cousin, scientist William Parsons, organised the construction of what was, at the time, the world's largest reflecting telescope—the Leviathan of Parsonstown—Ward made detailed sketches of the mighty instrument as it was being built. In the years after her death, these sketches were of critical importance in restoring the Leviathan of Parsonstown to its former glory.

Ward's interest in optics wasn't restricted to telescopes utilised to examine the heavens: she also made extensive use of magnifying glasses and microscopes in her study of things such as insects. Ward became so skilled with microscopes and preparing specimens for microscopic examinations that other scientists would commission her to aid them with their microscopy.

However, sadly but unsurprisingly, as a woman in science Ward had a very tough time of it, and despite her demonstrated expertise she was constantly turned away from universities and scientific societies. Her cousin, Parsons, aided Ward in exploring and expanding her scientific skills by connecting her with other scientists whom he knew and worked with, but she found it very difficult to make any great inroads into Britain's scientific community.

Ward did have some small successes, though: for instance, she managed to get herself on the mailing list for the Royal Astronomical

1 A good scientist, that is. The relative merits of her Irishness have never been conclusively determined.

Society, one of only three women on the list at the time.[2] Ward also wrote a great many books, most of them centred on microscopes and the worlds they revealed, but she had to self-publish them because—once again—as a woman, publishing houses weren't interested in her work. The setbacks Ward suffered were a terrible shame. Think about how many brilliant minds have been shunned and ignored over the millennia, think of all of the insights and knowledge we've missed out on, because of the terrible discrimination women used to face at the hands of men—and still do to this day, of course, especially in fields such as science.

In any case, Ward's career as a scientist was cut short by an untimely death that not only was tragic but also stands out as extremely unusual for the time period in which she lived.

The sons of her cousin William Parsons had built an experimental steam-powered car, something that never really caught on. Steam-powered cars faced a whole raft of problems. They were bulky and extremely heavy, and damaged roads that quite simply weren't designed for them. In 1865, the British government put a speed limit of 4 miles an hour on automobiles (that's just over 6 kilometres an hour, a brisk walking pace), which further hampered the development of the steam-powered car: why bother with the fuss of a car when you could walk at about the same speed? It wasn't until the modern

---

2 One of the other women was Mary Somerville, a Scottish scientist famous for her work as a mathematician and astronomer; the third was Queen Victoria, an English queen famous for her work as . . . well, a queen.

internal combustion engine was properly developed that cars were made viable, and back in 1869 that was still a good few years away.

All the same, one day the young Parsons boys took Ward and her husband along for a ride in their new invention, this steam-powered car. They were hooning around, presumably at a blistering 4 miles per hour—imagine that, being outstripped in a car by people out for a light jog—but sadly, whatever their speed, it was enough to bring about fatal consequences for Mary Ward.

While driving around a corner, poor Ward was thrown out of the car and fell under its wheels. As mentioned, steam-powered cars were *heavy*, so Ward was instantly crushed to death by its immense bulk. A doctor who happened to live nearby was swiftly summoned, but it was too late for him to do anything for Ward. Her death, as a result of this terrible event, meant that Ward became the first person ever to be killed in a motor-vehicle accident.

Today, fatal car crashes are far too common to be considered unusual, which is a damning fact in and of itself, but back in 1869, they were unheard of. So even if Mary Ward's death doesn't seem all that strange by today's standards, at the time it was completely unique.

34

Clement Vallandigham

Shot Himself as Part of a Legal Defence, 1871

Clement Vallandigham lived what can diplomatically be described as an interesting life, but he certainly had an even more interesting death. While working on the legal defence of a client on a murder charge, he accidentally—and fatally—shot himself. A fascinating legal tactic, to be sure, although not one that can be employed a second time.

Vallandigham was born in 1820 in Ohio, in the United States. After establishing a legal practice early in his career he left it behind to enter politics as a congressman in the time before the American Civil War. Unfortunately, he was firmly on the wrong side of history, being outspoken in his support of slavery: Vallandigham opposed the idea that the US federal government should have the power to regulate things such as slavery, which saw him exiled to the Confederate States of America. After a while, he ended up in Canada and ran for governor of Ohio remotely—he managed to win the Democratic Party nomination, although thankfully he lost the election.

He maintained his outspoken anti-abolitionist position throughout and even after the American Civil War, and went so far as to get involved in a Confederate conspiracy to overthrow the state governments of Ohio, Illinois, Indiana, and Kentucky. In short, he was a really nasty piece of work, and throughout the post-war Reconstruction period, he opposed any semblance of equality for African-Americans.[1]

In time, he ended up back in Ohio, where he lost enough elections to convince him instead to return to work as a lawyer. This proved to be a bad move, because it was while working as a lawyer that he died in truly bizarre circumstances.

In 1871, Vallandigham was defending a client named Thomas McGehean, who was facing a murder charge. McGehean was accused of shooting another man, Tom Myers, in the guts during a Christmas Eve bar-room brawl. In defending McGehean, Vallandigham came up with the idea of arguing that, rather than having been shot by McGehean, Myers had accidentally shot *himself*.

---

1 Although his hardline stance did soften somewhat towards the end of his life. Without wanting to give him too much credit, better late than never.

This wasn't as ridiculous as it sounds. Myers had been shot in the abdomen, so Vallandigham began to put together a scenario wherein Myers attempted to pull a pistol of his own from his pocket, firing before he managed to draw it fully. While pitching this idea during a meeting with other—perhaps sceptical—defence lawyers, Vallandigham decided that a demonstration was in order. After all, he was planning to re-enact the scenario before the jury in the courtroom, so a little rehearsal couldn't possibly hurt anyone.

Vallandigham picked up a pistol and put it in his pocket, then made a show of clumsily attempting to draw the pistol from his pocket, deliberately getting it caught on his clothing—just as Myers could have done. Then, just to really drive home the point, he actually shot himself in the stomach with it—just as Myers could have done.

This rather dedicated piece of method acting cost Vallandigham his life. Obviously, he didn't think that the pistol was loaded when he put it in his pocket, a misapprehension that was quickly dispelled by 1) a loud bang, and, shortly thereafter, 2) a significant amount of blood pouring out of his guts.

Vallandigham was rushed to some doctors, but it was no good. He was beyond saving, and died of his wounds the very next day. A sad and needless death, certainly, but you've always got to look for the silver lining. Thanks to Vallandigham's demise, McGehean's defence team now had incontrovertible proof that their line of argument was, in fact, feasible: you could indeed shoot yourself dead while fumbling to draw a pistol, and they had the corpse to prove it.

McGehean's murder trial went ahead, and you can only imagine how the defence team handled the case: 'Your Honour, we actually tested this ourselves, *very* thoroughly, and you'll never believe how it turned out . . .'

Amazingly, Vallandigham succeeded in successfully defending his client from beyond the grave. McGehean was eventually acquitted of his murder charge, perhaps aided by the defence having very convincingly proven that Myers *could* have shot himself after all. The defence presents to the courtroom Exhibit A: another bloke what did exactly the same thing, Your Honour.

35

Empress Elisabeth of Austria

Killed by a Loosened Corset (and Also, Admittedly, by the Assassin Who Stabbed Her Beforehand), 1898

A fascinating figure from nineteenth-century European history, Empress Elisabeth of Austria had a long, complicated, and unconventional career as a monarch after marrying Austrian emperor Franz Joseph I at the age of just sixteen. Nicknamed 'Sisi', she struggled to adjust to life in the Habsburg court, having difficulty with stiff imperial etiquette and a domineering mother-in-law,[1] but she eventually found her way and played a significant role in the history of the Austro-Hungarian Empire. However, her life was also filled with tragedy: one of her children died in infancy, and another was involved in a scandalous murder-suicide pact with his mistress.[2] Additionally, Elisabeth was extremely concerned with her appearance. Well into her later years, she starved herself half to death and wore extremely tight corsets so as to retain a youthful figure—and it was one of those corsets that was involved in her unusual death, although probably not in the way you would initially assume.

---

1 Archduchess Sophie, Franz Joseph's mother, was also Elisabeth's maternal aunt; Elisabeth upheld a proud and longstanding European royal tradition by marrying her cousin.

2 This scandal is known to history as the 'Mayerling Incident', which is a rather restrained name for a truly shocking affair—not to mention one with a significant historical impact. In November 1889, Sisi's son, 30-year-old Crown Prince Rudolf, began an affair with 17-year-old Baroness Mary Vetsera, the daughter of an imperial diplomat. A few months later, they were found dead in a hunting lodge in the village of Mayerling, just outside Vienna. While the Habsburg court tried to cover it up, it soon emerged that these star-cross'd lovers had decided they would rather die than break off their affair, and so had entered into a murder-suicide pact; Rudolf shot Mary, then turned the gun on himself.

The death of Rudolf, the only son and heir of Emperor Franz Joseph, triggered a succession crisis. Franz Joseph's brother renounced his claim to the throne, meaning the emperor's nephew became the heir apparent: his name was Archduke Franz Ferdinand, and he was famously assassinated in Sarajevo by Gavrilo Princip in 1914. Among the immediate consequences of this assassination was that the archduke never made it to the opening of the state museum later that day; incidentally, it also started the First World War.

In 1898, when Elisabeth was 60, she was on an incognito trip to Geneva, Switzerland. She was taking some time away from the stress of high office, focusing on wellness and relaxation, and as a result was doing everything she could to avoid the publicity and attention that often came with such a high-ranking imperial visit. However, a loose-lipped staff member at her hotel let it slip that the Empress of Austria was indeed staying there, so people in Geneva knew she was around.

This proved to be bad news for poor Sisi. A young anarchist named Luigi Lucheni was full of murderous political fury—knowing that various members of European royal and imperial families often holidayed in Geneva, he had travelled there with the express intention of killing a monarch. He didn't have a specific target in mind—any monarch would do, he wasn't fussy—and after discovering that the Empress Elisabeth was also there in the city, he decided that this provided him with the perfect opportunity to strike.

On the afternoon of 10 September 1898, Elisabeth was walking along the shore of Lake Geneva with a single lady-in-waiting, on her way to catch a steamship across the lake. As she walked, Lucheni approached and pretended to stumble while he was near her, bumping into the empress briefly before continuing on his way.

A moment later, Elisabeth collapsed, and not because she was overcome with a deep sense of tranquillity and wellness. Her lady-in-waiting raised the alarm, and Elisabeth was aided by a passing coachman as she got up and shakily walked the 100 metres or so to the steamship. Once aboard, she fell in and out of consciousness as the steamship set off, and so her lady-in-waiting opened her dress and cut the strings of her corset to allow her to breathe. This didn't seem to help much, however, and when the lady-in-waiting noticed a small, dark stain on Elisabeth's clothing, she went to the captain and had him turn the boat around and dock in Geneva once again.

Elisabeth was carried back to her hotel by six sailors who had made an improvised stretcher out of sailcloth and oars, but by the time they arrived, the empress was dead, with what was now clearly identifiable as a bloodstain spreading from her chest. This is, generally speaking, *not* the sort of outcome you're seeking when on a wellness retreat.

How did this happen? It was, as astute readers will no doubt have figured out,[3] due to the anarchist and avant-garde wellness consultant Lucheni. When he 'stumbled' into her, he actually stabbed her. He used a thin, 10-centimetre-long, razor-sharp blade that he had made himself; it was more or less a large needle. This blade had been stabbed into Elisabeth's chest, through a rib, a lung, and then into her heart.

But if that's the case, then *how* did she manage to walk 100 metres to board the boat? How did she not die instantly, bleeding out on the lake shore?

Because of her habit of dressing in extremely tight corsets! The corset she was wearing served to compress the wound to the point that the internal bleeding was slowed to a tiny trickle, her heart kept beating and, despite receiving what should have been a terrible wound, she didn't die immediately. But then, of course, she was taken aboard the steamship and her corset was loosened—and that was that for

3 Don't give yourself too much credit. It was in the chapter subheading.

Sisi. She began to haemorrhage internally and died just minutes later. Despite suffering what should have been an instantly fatal wound, Empress Elisabeth's habit of wearing tight corsets actually meant that she survived a fair bit longer than anyone might expect.

Lucheni, for his part, was discovered and arrested, and he confessed to the murder. He was open about his intent to kill a monarch—any monarch—for the cause of anarchy, and quite evidently hoped to be martyred for his deed: when he found out that capital punishment had been abolished in Geneva, he demanded to be tried elsewhere. Instead, he was sentenced to life imprisonment, although eventually got his wish of an early death. In 1910, he was found dead, hanged in his cell.

36

Jesse William Lazear

Deliberately Gave Himself Yellow Fever and Then Died, 1900

Jesse William Lazear was born in 1866 in the US city of Baltimore and received a first-rate medical education at institutes such as Johns[1] Hopkins University and the Columbia University College of Physicians and Surgeons, as well as further abroad in Paris, where he studied at the Institut Pasteur. In 1895, at The Johns Hopkins

1 'A typo! A typo!' the excited pedants exclaim. Well, *actually*, it is indeed Johns Hopkins University—Johns with an 's'. Johns Hopkins was a nineteenth-century US philanthropist whose fortune founded Johns Hopkins University and The Johns Hopkins Hospital. Bet you feel foolish now, hey?

Hospital, he began professionally investigating yellow fever, a viral disease most commonly spread by mosquitoes. In Lazear's home city of Baltimore, there was plenty of it to study.

While Baltimore these days is more closely associated with the hit TV series *The Wire* and people who have unusually strong opinions on seafood, historically the city (along with neighbours Philadelphia and New York City) was known for being a hotbed of yellow fever, playing host to deadly yellow-fever epidemics in the eighteenth and nineteenth centuries. Today, thanks to the wonder of modern vaccines, Baltimoreans don't have to concern themselves with yellow fever all that much, and instead they can concern themselves with finding strange new foods on which to put Old Bay seasoning.[2]

Back in Lazear's time, however, yellow fever was a much more pressing concern. During his time practising medicine in Baltimore, Lazear learned all he could about both this disease and malaria. Today, we know that both diseases are generally transmitted by infected mosquitoes when they bite people—yellow fever is the result of a viral infection, whereas malaria is due to a tiny unicellular parasite known as *Plasmodium*—but in Lazear's time, the cause behind the transmission of these diseases was unknown.

Their symptoms, though, were known all too well. Both yellow fever and malaria cause fever, chills, aches and pains, and can

2 A Baltimore institution, Old Bay is a seafood seasoning—but the manufacturers are oddly pushy about people putting it on stuff that isn't seafood. Weird Baltimoreans will insist that it's great when sprinkled on hot chips, pizza, cocktails, and even fruit.

eventually bring about severe jaundice as they attack the liver.[3] Every year, both diseases cause hundreds of thousands of deaths in less-developed regions of the world. Even with the advanced understanding we have of tropical diseases these days—a vaccine for yellow fever has been developed, and malaria is more preventable than ever—both of these diseases remain widespread and deadly.

Back when Lazear was researching them, yellow fever and malaria were among the most dangerous infectious diseases in existence, with epidemics of yellow fever in particular causing a devastating number of deaths not just throughout the tropics but also further from the equator, across Europe and North America—and specifically, as mentioned, in Lazear's home city of Baltimore. Lazear investigated yellow fever tirelessly in the waning years of the nineteenth century, and then, in 1900, he was given a brand-new opportunity to expand his studies and—just for good measure—help out old Uncle Sam in the process.

The Spanish-American War had recently ended, with the Americans giving the Spaniards a trans-hemispherical thrashing. This war resulted in the United States expanding its imperial ambitions by taking possession of the Philippines, Guam, and Puerto Rico.[4] The war also resulted, however, in a great many more US soldiers dying of yellow fever and malaria than at the wrong end of a Spanish rifle. Five times as many, in the end. The history books may tell us that

3 Yellow fever is so named due to the fact that severe jaundice can result in yellow skin.

4 The Philippines has since secured its independence, while Guam and Puerto Rico remain unincorporated territories of the United States.

the Americans beat the Spanish, but the real winners of the Spanish-American War were the mozzies.

It wasn't known at the time that mosquitoes were behind the spread of diseases such as yellow fever and malaria, which is a great pity. During the Spanish-American War, the United States lost fewer than 400 people to fighting, while Spanish combat deaths came in at around 750. In contrast, between the two sides, *17,000* men died from mosquito-borne disease. The United States would have been better served going after the mosquitoes rather than the Spanish, but then again, the mozzies didn't have a crumbling global empire that the United States could start to pick apart for themselves.

In the wake of the war, the Americans wanted to ensure that they never repeated the same mistake. They say that those who don't learn from the mistakes of history are doomed to repeat them: the United States would never again fight in any regionally based conflicts against a larger global foe in an effort to expand its international political and military influence only to lose countless men to the ravages of tropical diseases. Never ever.

Rather more proactively, US authorities back at the end of the nineteenth century wanted to find new ways to tackle tropical diseases such as yellow fever and malaria, and this is where Lazear came into his own. In 1900, he was offered the opportunity to travel to Cuba and work as a surgeon among the US military there, and to investigate just how a disease such as yellow fever was transmitted.

Fifty years previously, a man named Josiah C. Nott had hypothesised that insects were the culprits behind the spread of these tropical diseases. But before we congratulate Nott for this breathtaking bit of foresight, let's remember that it's just about the only thing he got right. Nott was an enthusiastic proponent of scientific racism, and maintained a personal collection of human skulls that he rigorously investigated in an attempt to prove his claim that intellectual capacity was governed by cranial size. Perhaps he was the one who needed his head examined.

In 1881, the idea of insect-borne disease was expanded by another epidemiologist, Carlos Finlay, who worked to demonstrate that mosquitoes, specifically, were behind the spread of yellow fever. Finlay, a man who sported the most magnificent set of mutton chops you could ever hope to see, was ridiculed mercilessly when he put his theory before his peers at the 1881 International Sanitary Conference. They didn't have time for this ludicrous idea about mosquitoes and yellow fever—they were likely too busy arguing about how filth built character, and how washing your hands was a gateway to moral decline.

Unperturbed by the vicious mockery of other epidemiologists, however, Finlay continued his pioneering work and is today recognised as a key figure in the understanding of vector-borne diseases—as, for that matter, is Lazear.

In Cuba, Lazear joined a dedicated team of medical experts known as the Yellow Fever Board, led by the famed Walter Reed, who had been commissioned to explore Finlay's 'mosquito hypothesis'. In time, the Yellow Fever Board would revolutionise the understanding of tropical disease by proving this once-maligned hypothesis to be true.

Lazear played a pivotal but unfortunately quite temporary role in this process. Wanting to test as directly as possible the theory that mosquitoes could spread yellow fever, he allowed himself to be bitten by an infected mosquito just to see what would happen next. While yielding valuable epidemiological insights, Lazear's methodology suffered from certain deficiencies in overall experimental design: namely, a lack of replicability, as the experiment's results duly killed him.

In truth, Lazear made a heroic sacrifice in the name of medical progress. At the age of just 34, he offered up his own life in search of scientific knowledge that would go on to save millions of other lives. Not that he was hailed as a hero at the time: Lazear's family actually covered up the fact that he had *allowed* himself to be bitten because otherwise their life insurance payouts would have been affected. Instead, they claimed that his death was accidental, and the truth of the matter wasn't revealed until Lazear's personal notes came to light in 1947.

Nonetheless, Reed was able to use Lazear's death—even spun as an accident—to gain more attention and resources for his team as they worked to prove the link between mosquitoes and yellow fever, and before long, this was accepted as scientific fact. While the disease is still prevalent and deadly in some parts of the world, the pioneering work of Finlay, Reed, Lazear, and everyone else who came together to fight yellow fever means that it claims a fraction of the lives it used to many years ago.

Reed very honourably laid the credit for his team's success at the feet of Finlay, who had been the first one to specifically suggest that mosquitoes were behind yellow fever.[5] Further, Reed also openly acknowledged the role Lazear had played: 'I lament his loss more than words can tell; but his death was not in vain. His name will live in the history of those who have benefited humanity.'

5 Reed does seem to have been a decent bloke. Not only was he a pioneer of biomedicine with his work on yellow fever, but he is also the first person in recorded history to have used a medical consent form as part of his experiments.

37

Bobby Leach

Died after Becoming the Second Person to Go Over Niagara Falls in a Barrel, 1911

The first person to go over Niagara Falls in a barrel was a woman named Annie Edson Taylor. She undertook this remarkable feat on 24 October 1901, on her *63rd birthday*, and did it hoping to make some money after falling on hard times. Amazingly, she survived, although the stunt didn't end up generating much wealth for her—she died penniless, twenty years later.

The *second* person to go over Niagara Falls—someone who heard about what Taylor did and somehow thought 'well, *that* sounds like good fun'—was a man named Bobby Leach. As his name is featured here as a chapter heading in a book entitled *History's Strangest Deaths*, you're probably already beginning to piece together how you think his story might end.

Leach was born in 1858, in Lancaster, England. At some point, he moved to the United States; while there, he worked as a performer for the famous Barnum & Bailey Circus. Established around 1870 by the American P.T. Barnum, the circus initially went by spectacularly unwieldy names such as 'P.T. Barnum's Travelling World's Fair, Great Roman Hippodrome and Greatest Show on Earth' before wisely trimming its name to just Barnum & Bailey, after Barnum merged his circus with another one belonging to a man named James Bailey. The Barnum & Bailey Circus was and still is very well-known for a great many things, including Jumbo the Elephant—it was the archetypical late-nineteenth-century circus, with wild animals and clowns and acrobats. And among its acrobats around the turn of the twentieth century was none other than Bobby Leach.

Leach performed brave and daring acrobatic stunts to adoring crowds, and as a performer he seemed to live by the motto 'anything you can do, I can do better'. For instance, he once watched another stuntman die a horrible death attempting to dive off a 4.5-metre-high diving board into water that was only 1.5 metres deep. Leach tried the same feat and somehow pulled it off, doing it better than the original stuntman in the sense that he didn't perish as part of the act.

Hearing about Annie Edson Taylor and her barrel ride over Niagara Falls, Leach decided that he once again had someone to outdo. He began to boast that he would show up Taylor and do what she had done, but better. How, exactly, his version of the stunt would be *better* remains a little unclear, but all the same Leach certainly was talking the talk about going over Niagara Falls in a barrel.

He didn't, however, seem to be in a great hurry to walk the walk: by the time he had actually made the preparations and was ready to perform the stunt himself, almost ten years had passed since Taylor's initial exploit. All the same, on 25 July 1911, Leach was found at the top of Niagara Falls with a custom-made metal barrel, ready at last to put his money where his mouth was.

Niagara Falls is just over 50 metres high. That's the length of an Olympic swimming pool, but it's difficult to visualise a swimming pool standing on its end, so instead think of Pisa's Leaning Tower (56.7 metres), London's Nelson's Column (51.5 metres) or Paris's Arc de Triomphe (50 metres). Sure, it's no Burj Khalifa (830 metres), but a fall from 50 metres will almost certainly kill you. The only sure-fire way to survive a 50-metre fall is to jump off something at least 51 metres tall.

While Niagara Falls has water at the bottom, which can be a little more forgiving as a landing surface than, say, pavement, going over the falls is still an extremely dangerous thing to do. Even today, a significant number of daredevils who try this end up dying. To make things worse, even if you do survive the stunt, the reward for your success will be a stiff fine from the cops.

In 1951, the daredevil William 'Red' Hill died while attempting a plunge over Niagara Falls, and in the wake of his well-publicised death, it was made illegal to attempt to go over the falls, no matter what personal watercraft you choose to use: boat, canoe, kayak, jet-ski, barrel, or, in Hill's specific case, a baker's dozen of inner tubes from truck tyres. If you make it over the falls in one piece, the Canadian authorities will get you for CA$10,000, while in the United States you'll get done for up to US$25,000. If you *must* go over the falls, swim over to the Ontario Provincial Police afterwards, rather than the New York State Troopers. It'll be cheaper that way.

Anyway—back in 1911, Leach was determined to see the stunt through, and that's just what he did. At the top of the falls, he clambered into his barrel and closed up its opening, before the barrel was pushed out into the Niagara River. The barrel slowly floated towards the waterfall's precipice, and then over it went: the barrel plummeted to the bottom, before finally emerging, bobbing out of the foam and spray towards the nervously waiting onlookers. The barrel was retrieved and opened, with people eager and excited to see if Leach had survived—had he actually pulled off his daring exploit?

You know what happened, don't you? The bloke who bragged about how he was going to go over Niagara Falls, the fellow who decided that he wanted the dubious honour of being the *second* person in history to go over the falls in a barrel—he's now being prominently featured in a book all about history's strangest deaths. You can guess what came next, can't you?

Yep, that's right: he slipped on an orange peel in New Zealand fifteen years later, injured his leg, got gangrene, and died.

38

Franz Reichelt

Died after Jumping off the Eiffel Tower with a Homemade Parachute, 1912

The aviation industry has had its fair share of famous pioneers, people who risked life and limb to take humankind into the air. The early days of aviation were very dangerous, much more so than other times during which humans made great technological leaps forward. Trial-and-error experimentation while banging rocks together might result in a sore thumb; trial-and-error experimentation while trying to fly might result in you doing an impressively accurate impression of a pancake. This was the ultimate fate of tailor and inventor[1] Franz Reichelt.

1 He was a lot better at one of these things than he was at the other.

Reichelt was born in 1878 in Bohemia, which is today part of the Czech Republic. At the age of twenty, he moved to Paris, where he worked as a tailor and dressmaker, finding success catering for wealthy Austrian visitors to the French capital, given his native German tongue.

However, in 1910, the world's interest in aviation started to well and truly pick up. Reichelt became very interested in developing a functioning parachute, which made sense given he worked with cloth every day. Parachutes, at that point, were nothing like they are these days. They weren't packed away in little backpacks—they were essentially enormous canopies that were already open, like a hang-glider with no rigidity.

This meant that they weren't the sort of thing you could wear while flying a plane. Reichelt's revolutionary idea was to make a suit that wouldn't be much bulkier than a regular flying outfit, but would automatically unfurl and safely deliver a pilot to the ground if they fell from their plane. Obviously, the idea caught on, as we have deployable parachutes even today, but sadly it wasn't Reichelt who got us there.

Reichelt worked away at the problem throughout 1910, having some initial success with mannequins wearing prototype parachute suits. He would test the suits by chucking these crash test dummies out of a window above the courtyard of the building in which he lived, but he couldn't overcome one key problem: the suits were far too heavy. His initial designs weighed around 75 kilograms, far too much for a pilot to wear while flying a plane. Quite aside from the weight problem, when he showed off his invention to aviation clubs, they weren't convinced that the parachutes would actually be strong enough to safely carry a pilot to the ground.

Unfortunately, the going got tougher for the unhappy Reichelt, as he started to hit more and more obstacles with his tests. He kept chucking dummies out of the window into the courtyard, but these tests resulted in more busted-up mannequins than successful parachutes.

But then, in 1911, a 10,000-franc prize was put on the line for anyone who could develop a safe parachute that weighed under 25 kilograms. The rich reward on offer inspired Reichelt to redouble his efforts to earnestly seek ways to reduce the weight of his parachute suit while increasing its overall surface area.

He sacrificed more dummies at the altar of his invention, but after a while, Reichelt wasn't satisfied with hoisting them out into the courtyard. He wanted to test them from a greater height. In that regard, he was in luck: Paris is home to the Eiffel Tower, which, back in 1911, was the tallest building on Earth at 312 metres.[2]

Reichelt applied to the Parisian police for permission to test his parachute suit from the tower's first deck, which is 57 metres off the ground. It took a long time and a lot of nagging, but eventually, in

---

2 A record it held from 1889 until 1930, when New York City's Chrysler Building finally overtook it, at 319 metres. Thanks to the addition of various broadcasting antennae, the Eiffel Tower is now 330 metres tall and so has overtaken the Chrysler Building, but these days doesn't even break into the top 100 of the world's tallest freestanding structures.

early 1912, the cops finally gave Reichelt permission. Reichelt was thrilled. At last, a proper chance to test the suit he'd been working on!

On the morning of 4 February 1912, Reichelt arrived at the Eiffel Tower with his parachute suit. Not just with it, either: *wearing* it. As it turned out, his plan had always been to test the suit personally by throwing *himself* off the tower. The police were taken aback because they'd given him permission on the understanding that he'd just be throwing another dummy; the crowd assembled to watch this unfold were similarly concerned for Reichelt's safety. As he ascended the Eiffel Tower with his true intentions made clear, many people attempted to talk Reichelt out of the stunt, but the determined tailor wasn't to be put off. He was sure he'd got the suit right this time. He was certain that it would work, and that he would not only be the talk of the town but also snag the juicy 10,000-franc reward.

At 8:22 a.m., after repeatedly rebuffing every single bit of resistance people offered to his plan as well as impassioned offers of a safety rope, Reichelt took his place on the first deck of the Eiffel Tower, proudly outfitted in his parachute suit, and stepped up onto the railing. He stood there very calmly, readying himself in the wind, and after hesitating for about 40 seconds, he finally launched himself off the tower . . . and fell straight to his death.

Reichelt's invention completely failed to break his fall. It didn't even open properly; instead, it just folded around him as he plummeted to the ground. He left a Looney Tunes-esque, 15-centimetre-deep impact in the frozen earth below. His mangled remains were taken to a hospital where he was officially—and altogether needlessly—pronounced dead.

Reichelt certainly achieved his objective of becoming the talk of the town—just not for the reason he was hoping. The next day's newspapers ran the story, and enraptured Parisians were utterly fascinated by the grisly details; the film taken of his jump was played in newsreels in the days afterwards. Rather than describe Reichelt as a 'mad genius', one French journalist suggested that only half the term could be accurately applied to him.

Still, to this day we remember Franz Reichelt. Even if he didn't secure the legacy he so strongly desired, history certainly hasn't forgotten him and his demise: an image of Reichelt is in pride of place, right at the top where everyone can see it, on the Wikipedia article entitled 'list of inventors killed by their own invention'.

39

Grigori Rasputin

Poisoned, Shot, Shot Again, then Thrown into a River Just to Make Sure, 1916

One of the most famous strange deaths from throughout history is that of Russian peasant turned imperial adviser Grigori Rasputin. It took multiple doses of cyanide, four bullets, and a frozen river to finally kill the seemingly indestructible Russian mystic.

Rasputin was born in 1869 as a peasant in Siberia, part of the Russian Empire. His early life was thoroughly unremarkable: he got married, had three kids, and worked on the family farm; nothing out of the ordinary. But then, in 1897, he went on a pilgrimage to St Nicholas Monastery in the little town of Verkhoturye and returned a changed man. He was filled with religious fervour, and began to gain followers of his own as a holy man and mystic.

His momentum as a new religious leader came to the attention of the Russian Orthodox Church and the Russian nobility in St Petersburg, and he was eventually introduced to Tsar Nicholas II and Tsarina Alexandra. He must have made quite an impression on them—while they'd been known to seek the guidance of unorthodox religious leaders in the past, Rasputin was almost immediately taken into their inner circle. This was probably because he claimed to be able to heal the imperial couple's young son, Alexei, of haemophilia. Rasputin already had a reputation as something of a faith-healer, and he put his skills to work with the young tsarevich.

Historians still argue to this day exactly what Rasputin did to achieve results that impressed the tsar and tsarina. He may have used peasant folk medicine ordinarily reserved for horses with internal bleeding; other suggestions include him dismissing medications prescribed by doctors that included aspirin, which wasn't known to be a blood-thinner back then. Whatever it was, Rasputin's treatment of Alexei secured his place in the imperial inner circle, and he became a constant companion of Nicholas and Alexandra.

Rasputin became more than a spiritual adviser, as well. He began to interfere in political affairs, and his influence over the tsar was not well regarded by the Russian nobility. This wasn't helped by some of his other habits. Rasputin would go out, get on the turps, sleep with a large number of women[1] and generally make a big nuisance of himself.

1 His wife didn't mind, apparently, saying he had 'enough for everybody'.

There were even rumours that he was also sleeping with the tsarina, although there's not much in the way of evidence for this.

Despite the disapproval of the Russian aristocracy, Rasputin's lofty position at the imperial family's side was more or less untouchable. He was constantly in the tsar's ear, boxing out the nobles and ministers who had advised and assisted the tsar before his arrival. As you can imagine, this only bred more resentment and hatred. Rasputin really wasn't a popular figure among the Russian upper classes.

With the Russian Empire crumbling after the outbreak of the First World War—Russian feudalism was falling apart, along with the economy—a cabal of nobles decided to rid themselves of this turbulent priest once and for all. They planned to assassinate Rasputin, hoping to then steer Tsar Nicholas back on course once his mystical, drunken, libertine holy man was out of the way.

The best record of Rasputin's assassination comes from the killer himself, a Russian nobleman by the name of Prince Felix Yusupov. After midnight on 30 December 1916, Yusupov invited Rasputin around to his palace, and when he arrived, Yusupov took Rasputin down to the basement and offered him some tea and cakes. Most hospitable, you might think—the cakes, however, had been laced with cyanide.

Rasputin munched them down, but he didn't seem to be in any bother at all. After finishing the poisoned cakes, he merely asked for some wine to wash them down. Deeply confused, Yusupov obtained some wine, which he also poisoned with cyanide, and watched as Rasputin drank three glasses. However, once again, he remained completely unaffected.

Yusupov scratched his head, wondering how this man could possibly still be alive after ingesting enough cyanide to kill a racehorse. It was 2.30 a.m., and Yusupov was now concerned about how he was going to get the job completed before dawn. He excused himself from the room and went upstairs to talk to some co-conspirators who were there, waiting for the deed to be done. Together, they decided that they'd have to take a rather more direct approach. One of them gave Yusupov a revolver, and off went Yusupov back down to the basement. He whipped out the gun and *blam*—he shot Rasputin in the chest. How uncivilised.

Rasputin collapsed to the ground, and Yusupov took Rasputin's coat and hat back to the conspirators. One of them put on these clothes and the others drove back to Rasputin's apartment, so people would think that the holy man got home safely. The conspirators then returned to Yusupov's palace and got ready to dispose of the body. Yusupov found Rasputin lying on the floor in the basement, just where he'd been left after being shot. But then, like a scene out of a horror film, the supposedly dead Rasputin leaped up and attacked Yusupov, filled with unbridled rage!

As you might expect, Yusupov just about shat himself, and fled at top speed back up to the other conspirators with Rasputin at his heels. Thinking quickly, one of the conspirators pulled out a gun and shot Rasputin again, and then again and *again*, just to make sure of it this time. Rasputin collapsed for a second time, but the conspirators weren't taking any chances. Fool me once, shame on you. Fool me twice . . . you can't get fooled again, Rasputin, because you're dead with four bullets in you, thank you very much.

Once the conspirators were certain that Rasputin was dead, they used fabric and rope to wrap up his corpse, drove it to a bridge, and dumped it through a hole in the ice that covered the Neva River. He wasn't coming back from *that*.

Rasputin's corpse was discovered under the river ice two days later, and an autopsy was carried out that night. The corpse had a bullet wound in the middle of the forehead, and there was no evidence of water in the lungs, so it's very likely Rasputin was indeed dead before he was unceremoniously chucked into the Neva. Furthermore, the doctor who conducted the autopsy didn't find any trace of poison in Rasputin's system, so this particular element of the story may have been a later invention of Yusupov as he retold the lurid tale in his 1928 memoirs. Incidentally, Yusupov and his co-conspirators were never arrested nor charged with any kind of crime for what they did. They quite literally got away with murder.

In any case, Rasputin was buried the day after his corpse was discovered, 2 January 1917, but that's not *quite* the end of the story. Months after the burial, his body was exhumed and burned by some soldiers so as to avoid his grave becoming a shrine, and also maybe—*maybe*—because they were still worried he might come back to life again.

The story of Rasputin's fascinating life and equally remarkable death has generated a lot of interest over the years. Even today, it's still a very famous story: the peasant who somehow became a trusted adviser to the Russian emperor himself, before being unsuccessfully poisoned, then shot, shot again, and dumped into a river, just to make bloody well sure he was dead.

40

King Alexander of Greece

Bitten by a Monkey, 1920

The most famous Alexander that the Greek world has ever produced is undoubtedly Alexander the Great, the famous king of Macedon. Born in 356 BCE, Alexander inherited his father's kingdom at the age of twenty, then spent his days forging one of the largest empires that history has ever seen, and his nights mostly getting on the grog with his men. Alexander the Great died at the age of just 32, from either malaria, typhoid fever, or just good old-fashioned poison; aside from dying relatively young, there was nothing particularly strange about the death of the most famous Greek Alexander. The *second*-most famous Greek Alexander, however, died in a way that, well, is probably the main reason he is remembered as the second-most famous Greek Alexander.

Alexander of Greece was born in 1893, the second son of the eventual King Constantine I of Greece. Constantine didn't fare well during the First World War, being forced into exile from Greece in 1917 due to his opposition to the Allied powers. After his father and the rest of his family were exiled, young Alexander took the throne—but as the Greek prime minister responsible for ousting Constantine, Eleftherios Venizelos, had the backing of the Allies and was essentially completely in charge of Greece, Alexander was reduced to a figurehead.

More or less a prisoner of Venizelos in his own palace, Alexander was politically ineffective and irrelevant, completely sidelined by the Venizelos administration as he was forced to rubber-stamp whatever government policies were put in front of him. He made the best of it, taking trips to the fronts to raise the morale of Greek troops, and enjoying the fact that Greece emerged in a pretty good position once the war was concluded—it had increased in size quite significantly thanks to the defeat and collapse of the Ottoman Empire, although the Greeks failed to recapture the ancient city of Constantinople.[1]

---

1 Today known as Istanbul, but, once again, that's nobody's business but the Turks'.

On a more personal level, Alexander was at the centre of a royal scandal when, in 1919, he descended from the lofty heights of his upper-class pedigree to marry a commoner, Aspasia Manos. He did this in contravention of the wishes of his family, the Greek Orthodox Church, and the Greek public at large—when the scandal broke, Aspasia left Greece for months so as to let people cool their heels for a while. She eventually returned, but was never named as queen and was forbidden from attending official events with her husband.

All the same, Alexander and Aspasia settled down together at the Royal Palace of Tatoi, just north of Athens. Sadly for the young couple, however, it was in the grounds of this royal estate that Alexander suffered an accident that would bring his life to an end—a life that was shorter even than Alexander the Great's.

On 2 October 1920, Alexander was wandering through the grounds surrounding the palace with his dog, Fritz, a German shepherd. It's not clear who started the altercation, but at one point Fritz got into a fight with another pet that was out and about in the grounds, an animal belonging to the steward of the palace vineyard: a Barbary macaque.[2]

The king intervened as these animals went at one another, attempting to drag the dog and the monkey apart. As it happened, however, the vineyard's steward hadn't restricted himself to keeping just one Barbary macaque, and while Alexander was occupied with

2 The *pet* was a Barbary macaque. According to most reputable accounts, the vineyard's steward was a human.

breaking up the fight between monkey and dog, a *second* macaque leaped into the fray and attacked Alexander, wounding him quite badly by chomping him on the leg. Alexander's attendants rushed over to chase the monkeys away, and swiftly called for aid for the king; his wound was treated, and he deemed that throughout this incident the worst injury he had suffered had been to his dignity. This was not correct. It was definitely the one to his leg.

Within hours, the bite wound was showing signs of infection. Alexander became feverish as sepsis set in, and the doctors that were summoned to treat the king regarded amputation to be the only way to save the king's life. However, none of them wanted to be the one responsible for hacking off a royal leg, and so no amputation took place. They didn't seem to have much of a Plan B, however, other than just hope His Majesty got better.

His Majesty did not. As the days turned to weeks, he became more and more unwell, his fever worsening to delirium. Shortly before the sepsis killed him, the unhappy Alexander started to call out for his mum, but Venizelos and the Greek government wouldn't hear of letting the exiled royals back into the country—and so, very sadly on 25 October, Alexander died surrounded not by friends and family, but by political enemies and prevaricating doctors. Alexander the Great conquered half the known world and died at the age of 32; Alexander the Potentially Appetising was bitten by a monkey and died at the age of 27.

Alexander's death triggered a minor succession crisis—his younger brother refused to accept the throne, and so in the end the ongoing embarrassment of having an empty throne forced the Greeks to ask King Constantine I to return from exile and take up the crown once more. Venizelos, furious with this result, exiled *himself*, trading places with the returned king. The political turmoil that came about with the restoration of Constantine greatly destabilised Greece and weakened its position in the ongoing Greco–Turkish War of 1919–1922. In the end, Greece lost this war with extremely heavy casualties—wartime leader and history's most quotable bigot Winston Churchill described the death of Alexander by saying 'it is perhaps no exaggeration to remark that a quarter of a million persons died of this monkey's bite'.

41

Frank Hayes

Died While Winning a Horse Race, 1923

It's very common for horse races to have winners; indeed, it's probably fair to say that most horse races are won by someone or other. This is very much the point of the sport.

Less common, however, is for jockeys to die on horseback, mid-race. It can happen—horse racing is a dangerous industry, and sadly there are many recorded instances of jockeys dying while racing. This is very much *not* the point of the sport.

There's only one jockey known to history, however, to have won a horse race while dying halfway through it. In 1923, a jockey named

Frank Hayes managed this unfortunate but very unique achievement, as his corpse rode to victory in a steeplechase.

Born in Ireland in 1901, Hayes immigrated to the United States while still young. On the other side of the Atlantic, he was able to find work as an equestrian trainer and stablehand. He didn't ordinarily work as a jockey, but in mid-1923 he got the opportunity to race at New York's famous Belmont Park and seized the chance with both hands. With the general need for jockeys to be small and light, Hayes first had to lose a fair bit of weight in order to race, but he was so eager for the gig that he worked extremely hard to shed 5 kilograms, and consequently was able to take to the track for the first time on 4 June. He rode a horse called Sweet Kiss—which you'll agree is certainly *quite* a name—and ran an absolute blinder, impressing the crowd with the way he handled the horse.

Hayes put on a real display: on overtaking the favourite, it looked like he was so confident of victory that he seemingly started to show off. He let go of the reins with one of his hands and slumped over in the saddle as though asleep, kind of like how victorious motorcycle racers do a cool wheelie as they're about to cross the finish line, except . . . well, slightly less impressive, to be honest.[1] After he had won the race, the horse's owner rushed over to congratulate Hayes, and you can only imagine her surprise in realising that Hayes wasn't showing off at all: he was stone dead.

1 Then again, horses can't really do wheelies, can they. Can they?

An attending doctor found that Hayes had had a fatal heart attack, probably brought on by his strenuous weight loss before the race and the excitement of overtaking the favourite and charging towards victory. It's unbelievable that the dead Hayes stayed on the horse for the remainder of the race, especially given that the steeplechase involves the horses jumping over obstacles, but he did, and so won the race, technically speaking.

A full and oddly poetic report of this bizarre incident was published the next day in the local newspaper, *The Auburn Citizen*.

> JOCKEY RIDES FIRST WINNER AND THEN DIES
>
> New York, June 5—Death clutched Francis Hayes, steeplechase jockey, after he rode his first winner yesterday at Belmont Park.
>
> Sweet Kiss, his mount, cleverly handled, came across the finish line a length in front of the favorite, Gimme, with the lad swaying from side to side.
>
> Hayes was valiantly but weakly tugging at the bridle as death gripped his heart and the mists swam before his eyes. Sweet Kiss cantered 100 yards further and stopped. The jockey crumpled in the saddle, slipped slowly over this mount's sides, fell face downward and lay still.
>
> Dr. John A. H. Voorhees, track physician, hurried to the fallen jockey.
>
> 'Heart disease,' was his comment.
>
> Did the excitement of riding his first winner, a joy so dear to all jockeys worth the name, prove too much for Hayes? Probably.

But he had also indulged in very strenuous work on the road in order that he might ride Sweet Kiss. He had reduced from 142 to 130 pounds[2] in the last few days.

Sweet Kiss was a well played second choice, at 5 to 1, and a great roar swept out when she came home first. It was a roar Hayes had often dreamed of. He had been permitted to drink in the joy of it yesterday as death came to him.

Quite aside from all the flowery language, you really do get the sense that the editor needed to fill some space in the newspaper that day. At the very least, you can tell that this article is a hundred years old. If it had been published today, its headline would have been: 'Jockey Rides First Winner and Then You Won't Believe What Happened Next!'

2 From 64 to 59 kilograms, for any readers not in the United States, Liberia, or Myanmar.

42

Michael 'Iron Mike' Malloy

Murdered—Eventually—as Part of an Insurance Scam, 1933

Michael Malloy worked very, very hard to stay out of this book. He was the victim of a great many bizarre attempts on his life, as a gang of crooks tried to knock him off so as to collect on multiple fraudulent life insurance policies, but he managed to survive all of them. Well, actually, all but *one* of them, technically speaking. Malloy shrugged off being poisoned, being frozen, and even being run over a couple of times, and his apparent indestructibility meant that he entered the history books with the very appropriate moniker 'Iron Mike'. In the end, these crooks *did* manage to find a way to bring Iron Mike down, but it wasn't easily done and meant that their get-rich-quick scheme ended up being anything but quick—and also, incidentally, didn't leave them rich for very long.

Michael Malloy was born in Ireland's County Donegal in 1873 and, like so many Irish people around this time, he left the Emerald Isle behind in the 1920s, crossed the Atlantic, and landed in the United States to seek his fortune. In New York City, Malloy worked in various jobs, including as a firefighter, but unfortunately he fell on hard times as the Great Depression took hold in the early 1930s. By 1932, Malloy was destitute and homeless, and had taken to the bottle to drown his sorrows. Malloy could be found in and out of bars every day, drinking himself half to death—but not, importantly to our story, all the way there.

The owner of one of these bars, a rather unscrupulous man named Tony Marino, took notice of Malloy's condition and his habits, and sniffed out an opportunity for himself. If Malloy is so determined to drink himself to death, Marino thought to himself, then why shouldn't I help him along—and earn myself a payday at the same time?

Marino had experience in this field: in 1931, he had pulled off a devilish piece of insurance fraud. Marino had befriended a woman named Mabelle Carson and tricked her into taking out life insurance that named *him* as the beneficiary, then killed her by getting her drunk, soaking her bed with cold water, and putting her in it next to an open window in the middle of winter. Carson was found to have frozen to death by the medical examiner—tragic, but not suspicious—and so Marino had collected on the life insurance policy he had tricked her into taking out.

Sensing an opportunity for a second helping at the insurance fraud buffet, Marino recruited three accomplices to aid him with the scheme: Joseph Murphy, Francis Pasqua, and Daniel Kriesberg. The men involved in this murderous plot would become known—for very good reason—as the Murder Trust, but it turned out they would have to work very, very hard to actually live up to the name.

The plot began one night when Malloy came into Marino's bar. Malloy, as usual, drank like a fish, wilfully encouraged by the Murder Trust's Murphy, who worked at the bar. Murphy made sure that Malloy was three sheets to the wind,[1] and then put a sheaf of papers in front of him, asking him for his signature on what Murphy claimed was a 'political petition'. Needless to say, it was *not* a political petition—it was a life insurance application form, which the plastered Malloy duly signed without noticing.

The form was then taken by Pasqua, who put the next stage of the plan into action. Using a corrupt insurance agent with the required moral flexibility for this scam, Pasqua went around with a friend

1 Here's something interesting: the saying 'three sheets to the wind', meaning extremely drunk, is a nautical term, but the 'sheets' in question aren't sails, as you might have thought—they're actually ropes. In the nautical world, a 'sheet' is a rope or cable that controls the sails, so 'three sheets to the wind' refers to when three of these ropes are loose, blowing in the wind, presumably resulting in a ship that is out of control, like a drunk person might be.

of his who posed as Malloy in a series of meetings with insurance companies.[2] With Malloy's signature and this impostor pretending to be him, Pasqua managed to take out *three* separate life insurance policies, the premiums all paid for by the conspirators in anticipation of the returns they would receive after Malloy's death.

With the insurance policies signed and sealed, the Murder Trust could have been forgiven for thinking the hard part was over. After all, they only had to knock off an old drunk now and they'd pocket thousands of dollars in insurance payouts as soon as they killed Malloy—and how hard could *that* possibly be?

The next time Malloy appeared in Marino's bar, ready for another day of heavy drinking, he was delighted when Murphy told him he had an unlimited tab. All his drinks were on the house! Not one to ask too many questions or look a gift horse in the mouth, Malloy didn't waste any time in sinking shots like his life depended on it—when, in reality, the opposite was true. Murphy kept refilling Malloy's glass, and Malloy kept putting 'em away, but despite ending up as pissed as a newt, he very uncooperatively refused to pass out. He just drank and drank and drank before eventually staggering out of the bar, leaving Marino and his accomplices at a loss for words.

Their plan had been for Malloy to drink so much that he would die of alcohol poisoning, but aside from ending up absolutely blind drunk, Malloy seemed to be none the worse for having drunk half

2 To this day, the identity of the man who pretended to be Malloy remains a mystery.

the bar. It's not like the Murder Trust could take advantage of Malloy's drunken condition to take him somewhere while incapacitated and just, like, shoot him. That would probably come up in the autopsy.

No: it had to look like an accident, the sort of unsuspicious death an unfortunate old drunk like Malloy would suffer. The conspirators, therefore, decided to give the alcohol poisoning a helping hand the next day. Malloy returned to Marino's bar, hoping for another day's worth of free drinks, and when he found out that was exactly what was on offer, he was as happy as a pig in shit. This time, however, Murphy was serving up Malloy's drinks with a special little ingredient that had an extra kick: engine coolant.

Engine coolant is used, unsurprisingly, to keep a car engine cool. When added to a cooling system, its primary ingredient, ethylene glycol, raises the boiling point of the liquid inside the system. Marino and his gang, however, wouldn't have referred to this substance as engine coolant: as they were American, they would have called it antifreeze. Ethylene glycol doesn't just raise a liquid's boiling point, it also, somewhat confusingly, lowers a liquid's freezing point.[3] One of the other amazing properties of this incredible chemical compound is that it will likely kill you if you drink it.

---

3 Most Australians generally don't have to worry about their engines freezing, however, so in Australia antifreeze is usually referred to as engine coolant. There are a *lot* of automotive articles and videos patiently explaining to the confused Australian motorist that antifreeze and engine coolant are, indeed, the same thing.

Lacing Malloy's drinks with the very toxic ethylene glycol found in engine coolant (or antifreeze, for those of a more northern hemispherical persuasion) should have been lethal, particularly in such high concentrations. Malloy, by rights, should have keeled over, dead of ethylene glycol poisoning, after a few mouthfuls of the stuff. He didn't, however, for a truly fascinating reason.

It may sound amazing that ethylene glycol can, simultaneously, protect liquid from both extreme heat and extreme cold, but no one is likely to be surprised by the fact that a substance with such a crunchy chemical name is a deadly poison. You might be surprised by one of the antidotes to ethylene glycol poisoning, however—an antidote that, as it just so happens, Iron Mike Malloy was chock-full of: *alcohol.*

Unbelievably, alcohol counteracts the toxic effects of engine coolant: the ethanol present in alcohol prevents the liver from absorbing ethylene glycol into the bloodstream. Given how much booze was in Malloy's system, the deadly engine coolant didn't touch him in the slightest. Ignorant to the intricacies of the chemical relationship between ethylene glycol and ethanol, Murphy had effectively been serving Malloy doses of poison mixed with antidote.

When this attempt at poisoning Malloy failed, the Murder Trust moved on to different substances, becoming increasingly inventive—or, rather, increasingly desperate—in their quest to kill Malloy without raising suspicion. As the days passed, and as Malloy returned again and again to Marino's bar for round after round of free drinks, the conspirators experimented with a great many different additives. Turpentine was ineffective, as was equine liniment—a heat rub for horses—and even fortifying Malloy's drinks with a stiff dose of rat poison failed to affect Malloy in the slightest.[4]

At this point, the Murder Trust were starting to lose their patience. Over the next few days, they stopped with the pretence of serving Malloy liquor laced with poison, and instead did away with the liquor and just served him poison, neat. Murphy began to serve Malloy shots of straight, unadulterated *wood alcohol*, also known as methanol. Drinking even a small amount of methanol can cause blindness, and it doesn't take much more to kill you.

Malloy, however, started to cheerfully put away shots of wood alcohol, not even noticing it wasn't the whiskey he'd been drinking up to this point. It was, once again, this whiskey that saved him: just as with ethylene glycol, alcohol can counteract methanol poisoning, too. Malloy remained unaffected by the wood alcohol; these would-be killers were tripping over their own feet in trying to bring about the end of the seemingly indestructible Irishman.

Now utterly desperate, the group tried everything they could think of. Pasqua claimed to have seen a man die after eating oysters while drinking whiskey; so they soaked some oysters in wood alcohol and gave them to Malloy. He gratefully accepted, not believing his luck—free food, to go with all of these free drinks—and, once again, he suffered no ill effects.

It's at this point that the Murder Trust seems to have arrived at the 'no bad ideas' stage of their plot, because the next thing they

---

4 It doesn't seem that alcohol is an antidote to rat poison. However, this isn't a scientific investigation that you're encouraged to undertake yourself.

served up to Malloy was a sandwich filled with rotten sardines. At first blush, this seems a lot less lethal than something like engine coolant or wood alcohol, and the conspirators evidently thought so, too, as they added a healthy pinch of rat poison to the sandwich as well. In case that wasn't enough, however, they also hid *carpet tacks* in the sandwich, like they were Looney Tunes cartoon villains. It was an utterly ridiculous way to try to kill someone, and, as it turned out, an utterly ineffective one. Malloy happily devoured the sandwich, before returning to the booze—or, rather, the undiluted methanol—licking his chops after a delicious meal of rotten sardines and carpet tacks.

It was beginning to look like Iron Mike Malloy had an endless tolerance to, well, everything, from horse liniment to carpet tacks. The gang would have to try something different.

Initially, Marino hadn't wanted to freeze Malloy to death. This was how he had killed his first victim, Mabelle Carson, and he thought it might be suspicious to collect on *two* life insurance policies brought about by hypothermic deaths. The group was running out of options, however, and so decided to return to Marino's tried-and-true method.

The next time Malloy came into the bar, he was plied with enough alcohol for him to pass out on the floor. Under the cover of darkness, the conspirators then dragged Malloy outside into the freezing cold winter's night, dumped him in an empty park, soaked him with water, and left him to freeze to death. Once more, however, Malloy survived: he was found passed out in the snow by the police, who took him to a homeless shelter where he warmed up and slept off the drink. The very next day, sure enough, he was back drinking at Marino's bar again.

Far from bringing about a windfall for Marino and his gang, Malloy was doing the opposite. Not only was he drinking his way through all the alcohol in the bar, but there was also the cost of the antifreeze, turpentine, horse liniment, and wood alcohol to consider—not to mention the oysters![5] The Murder Trust needed Malloy dead before he bankrupted them, so they decided that desperate times called for desperate measures.

Abandoning all pretence, they added a new member to their ranks: a cab driver named Hershey Green. After another night of heavy drinking saw Malloy pass out in the bar, they loaded the Irishman into Green's taxi. Green drove to a quiet part of town, unloaded Malloy's unconscious body, and then ran over him with the car.

Twice. Just to be sure.

Driving off and leaving Malloy's mangled body, the gang was convinced that this would, finally, be the end of things. A drunken Malloy, tragically struck down by a careless driver, oh yes, very sad, such a shame—now, what about those life insurance payments?

The conspirators kept a close eye on the death notices in the newspapers, waiting to spot Malloy's among them; however, as the days turned into weeks, no such notice was printed. Confusingly, though, Malloy failed to appear at Marino's bar, so the Murder Trust were left wondering what could possibly have happened. After three weeks, they had their answer, when Malloy walked back into the bar, chipper as ever, ready to wet his whistle after a few weeks in hospital. He had

5 The rotten sardines and carpet tacks presumably didn't make too much of a hole in the budget.

been busted up after being hit by a car, he said, but was now all rested up and good to go—how about a drink, then?

By now, the Murder Trust had lost all patience. In addition to all of the expenses they'd had to bear already, this whole affair had gone on so long that they were now starting to be on the hook for monthly insurance premium payments. They resolved to murder Malloy come hell or high water, and see the job through to its conclusion this time. Malloy was once again served alcohol until he passed out, before being dragged back to Murphy's room. There, a hose attached to a gas jet was put in his mouth, while his nose was covered with a towel to force him to breathe from the hose.

At long, long last, it was this—not the booze or the engine coolant or the turpentine or the horse liniment or the oysters or the wood alcohol or the rotten sardines or the carpet tacks or the freezing or the being run over twice—that was finally enough to kill Iron Mike Malloy.

With Malloy finally dead, the Murder Trust paid off a crooked doctor to issue a false death certificate that stated Malloy had died of pneumonia, and orchestrated a swift burial before too many questions could be asked. Then, armed with their fraudulent death certificate, the gang went to finally collect on the life insurance policies they'd taken out—and, believe it or not, the insurance companies accepted the claims, deemed Malloy's death unsuspicious, and duly paid them out. The schemers got their payday, at last!

Their good fortune was extremely short-lived, however. By now, the police had caught wind of this supposedly indestructible Irishman who was a regular at Marino's bar, and after hearing of his death and the connected insurance payouts, they began to grow suspicious. The authorities exhumed Malloy's corpse and subjected it to a full autopsy; they found that Malloy had *not* died of pneumonia after all, and that his death was no accident.

The police tracked down the five members of the Murder Trust, arrested and questioned them, eventually unravelling the full story behind the plot to kill Malloy. All five were found guilty of murder, and four of them were sentenced to death (Green, the cab driver, received a life sentence). In mid-1934, the original members of the Murder Trust were sent to the electric chair, executed for the death of Iron Mike Malloy in New York City's infamous Sing Sing Prison.[6] Had Iron Mike ended up in Sing Sing's electric chair, however, you'd have to imagine that he would have caused a blackout across New York City before the chair actually had a chance to kill him.

6 Sing Sing Prison also provided us with the saying 'sent up the river'—as Sing Sing is upriver from New York City, convicted criminals sentenced to serve time in Sing Sing were said to have been sent up the river.

43

Thomas Midgley Jr

Strangled While Getting Out of Bed, 1944

The inventor and engineer Thomas Midgley Jr might be the single most environmentally destructive person ever to have lived. He has some stiff competition, of course, as his damaging inventions have to go up against things such as single-use plastic, the internal combustion engine and, you know, *nuclear weapons*, but Midgley gave it a red-hot go. His legacy speaks for itself: he was behind not one but *two* innovative pieces of technology that proved to be so harmful to the natural world that today they're banned more or less everywhere worldwide.

Midgley was born in 1889 in the US state of Pennsylvania, and he quickly showed an aptitude for invention. This was unsurprising, as both his father and grandfather had been inventors, although all they'd managed to create were things such as new types of car tyres and wood saws—nothing that involved the wanton destruction of the planet's environment. Nice try, though.

Given his interest in invention and engineering, Midgley attended the prestigious Cornell University,[1] where he earned a degree in mechanical engineering in 1911. A few years later, he landed himself a job at General Motors and became engrossed in attempting to solve an ongoing problem with which the nascent automotive industry was struggling.

Cars back then would often suffer from 'engine knock', where fuel in the engine would ignite at the wrong time. This was a problem that manifested itself in a couple of different ways: it could disrupt the smooth and efficient operation of a car, or it could cause the car to explode. As neither of these outcomes was ideal for the average driver, car manufacturers everywhere were desperately searching for a way to eradicate engine knock.

Luckily for them—and unluckily for just about every other life form on the face of the planet—Thomas Midgley came along with an inventive new approach to solving this problem. What he did was this: he picked up a periodic table and started to add elements one at a time to petrol, just on the off-chance that one of these elements would do

1 You'll find Cornell proudly listing people such as Ruth Bader Ginsburg, Anthony Fauci, and Bill Nye the Science Guy among its notable alumni, but you *really* have to dig into the archives to find any mention of Thomas Midgley Jr.

something about engine knock. If he had started with hydrogen and then continued down the list numerically, he would have had a very interesting time indeed, especially when he arrived at things such as sodium and potassium—pure potassium is so reactive that it explodes when exposed to *water*, never mind fuel—while he would have very likely ended up with some excitingly lethal chemical cocktails if he had tried things such as chlorine or phosphorus.

Amazingly, however, this brute-force approach did actually solve the problem of engine knock. Admittedly, it was a shame that the element in question just so happened to be lead, one of the more dangerously toxic elements, but Midgley wasn't going to let that stand in the way of progress.

After Midgley discovered its automotive applications in 1921, lead caught on like wildfire. It became a fixture in the fuel additive market, making engine knock a thing of the past. No longer were cars exploding due to engine knock, and the small price to pay for this was car exhausts spewing lead into the atmosphere—happily, that was a problem for future generations.

However, even back then, lead's toxicity was reasonably common knowledge. Having too much lead in your system[2] can bring about lead poisoning, the symptoms of which range from headache and memory loss right through to coma and death. Even when it doesn't kill you, lead poisoning is commonly associated with a reduction in cognitive function and antisocial behaviour. It's not nice.

---

2 Which is to say: any lead at all.

And it's also not new: lead poisoning is known to have plagued ancient Romans, who used lead to make their plumbing pipes[3] as well as to make jewellery and weapons. Interestingly, after the tomato was introduced from the Americas to Europe in the sixteenth century, it's thought that people considered tomatoes to be poisonous, when the real culprit was the pewter plates off which they were eating the tomatoes—the natural acidity of the tomato leached lead out of the pewter, causing nasty cases of lead poisoning and not, as people falsely assumed, tomato poisoning. Unless you're a horse, you're unlikely to fall victim to tomato poisoning.

Given the known dangers of lead poisoning in humans, however, General Motors cunningly marketed Midgley's new product without using the word lead. Instead, they used sanitised and euphemistic terms such as 'ethyl' or 'TEL', taken from the technical, chemical name of the liquid compound Midgley had found was so effective in dealing with engine knock: tetraethyl lead.

General Motors sent pro-lead lobbyists to sway lawmakers, covered up the adverse effects that exposure to lead was having on its workers, and swept damaging reports about the health hazards of leaded fuel under the rug, while Midgley was wheeled out to convince the public that 'ethyl' was perfectly safe. He took part in bizarre publicity stunts such as breathing in the fumes from tetraethyl lead and even using it to wash his hands, all to persuade people they had nothing to fear from leaded petrol.

---

3 This is where the term 'plumbing' comes from: *plumbum* is the Latin word for lead.

For eliminating engine knock, Midgley was hailed as a scientific hero; for his pioneering work, he received accolades, awards and—as a special bonus—a very bad case of lead poisoning. In 1923, he had to stop work altogether to recover, a luxury that workers producing tetraethyl lead at GM facilities didn't have, resulting in many deaths from lead poisoning. At least they would have had a nice, smooth, engine-knock-free ride in the hearse.

General Motors and the automotive industry more broadly did a very good job of keeping lead in petrol for a long time, even as more and more scientists came forth with damning reports about its danger and the extent to which it was poisoning the air. In the 1970s, governments finally began phasing out leaded fuel—but it's only very recently that atmospheric lead levels have finally fallen back down to around pre-Midgley levels. In the interim, countless people around the world suffered from lead poisoning, and even today older generations have hundreds of times the normal concentration of lead in their bloodstream.

But even after eliminating engine knock, Midgley wasn't yet finished; there was more destruction for him to wreak. He—sensibly—moved away from lead, never exposing himself to it when he could help it. General Motors shifted him to what was back then one of their subsidiary companies, Frigidaire, to work on refrigerators. This gave Midgley an all-new opportunity to invent another catastrophically damaging chemical.

Before Midgley, fridges used substances that were either poisonous, flammable, or both to keep the things inside them cool. Midgley's job was to find a new substance, one that wasn't so dangerous, to use as a coolant. And, in classic Midgley fashion, he managed to solve this problem very efficiently, concurrently setting in motion a global environmental disaster. The man was nothing if not consistent.

In 1928, Midgley invented dichlorodifluoromethane, usually (and mercifully) referred to as Freon, which became the world's first chlorofluorocarbon, or CFC. When it comes to fridges, CFCs are brilliant—they're not toxic, they don't burn, and they work exceptionally well as refrigerants. Even better, they can also be used as propellants for aerosols in spray cans!

It wasn't long before this miraculous new chemical concoction was being produced in vast quantities. By 1935, over eight million Freon-filled fridges had been sold across the United States, and that was just the start. Freon was being used in air conditioners and aerosols, it had applications as an industrial solvent, and, best of all, it wasn't hazardous to human health. Midgely even got up to his old tricks, putting on public demonstrations to show everyone just how safe Freon was: he would breathe in a great lungful of the stuff to prove it was non-toxic, then blow out candles to prove it was non-flammable.

Needless to say, Freon and other CFCs took the world by storm, being bunged into cooling systems and aerosols everywhere, just as lead petrol was bunged into cars everywhere. The parallels between these two substances are ridiculous: they were both invented by the same guy as he sought to alleviate a relatively minor engineering problem, and they both went on to have utterly disastrous consequences for the planet.

CFCs don't break down. The molecules farted out by a spray can full of CFCs hang around in the atmosphere for a long, long time—between 50 and 150 years—and eventually float into the upper atmosphere, which just so happens to be filled with their favourite food: ozone. A single chlorine atom from a CFC molecule can chew through *100,000* molecules of ozone. By the 1980s, CFCs had opened up a gaping hole in the ozone layer,[4] leaving Earth's surface much less protected from the sun's harmful rays.

Like tetraethyl lead, CFCs were banned and have been phased out of use, and thankfully the ozone layer is repairing itself. The ozone layer is miraculously self-regenerating: ultraviolet rays from the sun react with oxygen molecules in the atmosphere to create ozone through a photochemical process known as the Chapman cycle. All the same, repairing all the damage CFCs have done to the ozone layer is going to take a long time—atmospheric ozone concentrations won't be back to their pre-Midgley levels until around 2070. Long, long after his death, Midgley's legacy is still acutely felt by the natural world.

But how did he die? Well, believe it or not, even after his invention of CFCs, Midgley *still* wasn't finished with destructive inventions. His final invention, however, was destructive on a very different scale—rather than posing a broad danger to the world's natural environment, it posed a very specific danger to him, personally.

---

4 This hole opened up above Antarctica, with the thinning ozone extending as far north as Australia. Cheers for that, Midgley, mate.

In 1940, aged just 51, Midgley was afflicted with polio, and with it came a set of significant physical disabilities. The ever-ingenious Midgley, however, refused to compromise his personal mobility, and so devised a clever system of ropes and pulleys that would allow him to lift himself out of his bed, rather than require the assistance of others.

And, in the end, this device lifted him not just out of his bed but also right off this mortal coil altogether. On 2 November 1944, Midgely was found caught up in the ropes of his device, having been strangled to death by them—adding one final tally mark to the combined death toll of all of his disastrous inventions.

44

Mary Reeser

'Spontaneously Combusted', 1951

As ridiculous as it sounds, spontaneous combustion is a real thing. If something with a low enough ignition temperature manages to generate enough heat, it can just burst into flames by itself. This process has been observed to take place in, for instance, piles of hay and compost heaps. However, despite being neither a pile of hay nor a compost heap, 67-year-old American grandma Mary Reeser also seems to have spontaneously combusted back in 1951.[1]

1 She *seems* to have, but almost certainly didn't. But it's a terrific hook for this chapter, isn't it?

The death of Mary Reeser baffles experts to this very day and has never been fully or properly explained, despite extensive investigation. While her death has been scrutinised for decades, not much is known about her life. She was originally from a town called Columbia, in Pennsylvania, before moving to the Floridian town of St Petersburg after the death of her husband so she could live closer to her son, Richard, and his daughters.

On the night of Reeser's death, Richard had paid her a visit in her apartment. He had left at about 9 p.m., not knowing that his poor old mum would never be seen alive again. The next morning, Reeser's landlady knocked on her door to deliver a telegram. There was no response, and she noticed that the apartment door felt warm, while the door handle was burning hot—too hot to touch. Concerned, the landlady called the authorities, and firefighters forced their way into Reeser's apartment. When they broke through the door, they came upon a bizarre and utterly mystifying scene.

In the middle of Reeser's apartment was a pile of smouldering ash and cinders, and found in this pile were a burned human skull and some vertebrae, a handful of blackened teeth and, unbelievably, half of Reeser's lower left leg with the foot still in its shoe.

Even more extraordinarily, much of the rest of the apartment was unburned! Surrounding the ash pile were telltale signs of a fire that had burned with great heat and intensity, but aside from one part of a wall that had burned out, there were only small hints of the blaze that had occurred: plastic objects were slightly melted and malformed, unburned wicks sat in puddles of the wax that used to be candles, and smoke and soot stains were found across the ceiling and upper walls. However, other areas of the apartment bore no evidence of fire: most of the furniture was completely undamaged, Reeser's bedding was still pristine, and there were even unburned newspapers lying here and there.

This was incomprehensible. Reeser had, for no readily apparent reason, been burned to ashes in an extremely intense fire, while her very flammable surroundings were unscathed.

The police came to investigate, of course, but soon realised this was a case beyond the capacity of a local police department. So, they called in the FBI, writing to director J. Edgar Hoover:

> We request any information or theories that could explain how a human body could be so destroyed and the fire confined to such a small area and so little damage done to the structure of the building and the furniture in the room not even scorched or damaged by smoke.

This escalation did very little to clear up the mystery, and even today, the best explanations that have been put forward to account for this mystery are unproven. A lightning strike was dismissed, as fuses in the apartment didn't blow and the electrics showed no damage other than that caused by the heat of the fire. One supposed witness claimed to have seen a ball of fire descend from on high and hit Reeser through her open window, but evidence of this scenario was a little thin on the ground.

In saying that, there was about as much evidence for a ball of fire as there was for basically every other theory put forward, which is to say not very much at all. It really did seem like Reeser had spontaneously combusted. There are plenty of pseudoscientific whackos who believe that spontaneous human combustion is real,[2] but the investigators weren't about to cop out and use that as an explanation.

They were right in choosing not to: spontaneous human combustion has been thoroughly investigated and comprehensively debunked as pseudoscientific claptrap. Overwhelmingly, alleged instances of spontaneous human combustion have perfectly reasonable explanations, especially when it emerges that the supposed victim, for instance, fell asleep while drunk in front of a lit fireplace. But no, say the crackpots—it couldn't possibly be people getting pissed, passing out, and catching fire. It must be spontaneous human combustion.

Interestingly, the fact conspiracy theorists have latched onto spontaneous human combustion as yet another thing that the omnipotent and ever-malignant 'they' are trying to cover up has meant that ordinary people have started to disbelieve in actual, real spontaneous combustion—which, as clarified at the beginning of this chapter, is a real thing that does happen. Just not to humans.

Spontaneous combustion wasn't the only wild theory put forward to explain the demise of Mary Reeser—some suggested she had been the victim of a napalm or white phosphorus attack, for example—but the FBI settled on the theory they deemed to be the most plausible.

---

2 It isn't.

While it may have been plausible, it was still absolutely bonkers: investigators concluded that Reeser had taken her sleeping pills for the night and then settled into her armchair for one last cigarette before bed. She had fallen asleep with the cigarette still burning, which had set fire to her and caused her body fat to act as a fuel source, a process referred to as the 'wick effect'. Apparently, Reeser's chair sat upon a concrete floor, so the fire couldn't spread further throughout the apartment, so this theory covered the facts.

Well, *most* of them, at least. It didn't explain how such a fire could almost completely cremate a human body and reduce it to ashes, a process that requires the heat to be 800–1,000 degrees. A full-blown house fire doesn't always reach that sort of temperature, and to this day it's not understood how Reeser could have gone up in flames that were hot enough to melt the plastic around the apartment without setting the rest of the room on fire.

45

Margaret Wise Brown

Died While Demonstrating to Nurses Just How Healthy She Was, Thank You Very Much, 1952

There's a certain subsection of readers who will instantly recognise the name Margaret Wise Brown: those who have read—or had read to them—the classic 1947 children's bedtime story *Goodnight Moon*. However, for all its critical acclaim as one of the best picture books ever created, *Goodnight Moon* truly is a ludicrous publication.

The story, which involves the pre-bedtime rituals of an anthropomorphised rabbit as it prepares to go to sleep, features numerous laughable inaccuracies. For instance, two (non-anthropomorphised) cats are commonly featured in the illustrations, alongside a small mouse; at one point in the book, the cats are playing with a ball of wool while the mouse looks on in interest. In what world would that mouse not *immediately* scurry to safety? In what world would the cats not *immediately* abandon the wool and instead go on the hunt, seeking the blood of this scampering rodent, their ancient prey?[1]

Goodnight Moon doesn't just grossly misrepresent feline predatory behaviour; it also presents a wildly inaccurate understanding of planetary and lunar physics. According to astrophysicist Dr Chad Orzel, the only way to reconcile the rate at which the moon rises through the window with the time shown passing by the clocks in the book's illustrations is for the anthropomorphised rabbit's bedroom to be moving at around 99 per cent of the speed of light, which would have relativistic time dilation account for the discrepancies between the movement of the moon and the clock's hands.

Needless to say, it's exceedingly unlikely for anthropomorphised rabbits to possess technology that enables them to travel at such velocities.

Its innumerable flaws aside, *Goodnight Moon* has remained a popular and beloved piece of children's literature for over 70 years, and it's not the only book for which Margaret Wise Brown is remembered. She also authored *The Runaway Bunny* and *My World*, both of which are similar to *Goodnight Moon* in that they prominently feature anthropomorphised rabbits in a host of thoroughly improbable

1 And why—why oh why—does a family of *rabbits* keep predators such as cats as pets?

situations. All the same, Brown is celebrated as a successful children's author, and her works are still in print to this day.

Brown was born in the United States in 1910 and was educated in both fancy American private schools and fancy Swiss boarding schools. She worked as a teacher and an artist, and began writing children's books in the 1930s. This led to her working directly with a publishing company as an editor, and one of the projects she worked on while in this position was inviting established, well-known authors to write children's books. Sadly, this project didn't reach its full potential: despite reaching out to authors such as John Steinbeck and Ernest Hemingway, they never showed much interest in children's literature. A great pity! Imagine if Hemingway, rather than Brown, had written *Goodnight Moon*:

> The room was dim. It hurtled through the cosmos at an untold velocity. A small rabbit sat in bed. 'Goodnight, room,' he said. His eyes moved, studying the objects in his view. 'Goodnight, moon. Goodnight, stars.' The words were brief and sparse, like the ticking of a clock. On the floor, two cats inexplicably forsook a mouse for a ball of wool. 'Goodnight, kittens. Goodnight, mittens.' Against the cosmic turmoil, the room embraced the silence. The rabbit closed his eyes, surrendering to the warp of night, lost in the quiet hum of the unknown.

Brown had a reasonably successful career as an editor, but left this position behind in 1942 to focus on writing. She authored numerous works throughout the 1940s—including *Goodnight Moon*—and her reputation as a children's author grew and grew. In total, Brown wrote over a hundred books for kids, and this number would likely have been a lot higher had her life not come to an untimely and somewhat unexpected end.

While travelling in France, Brown became extremely unwell and was ultimately admitted to hospital for emergency surgery when her appendix ruptured. The surgery, happily, was a success: despite the potential lethality of appendicitis, Brown made it through in one piece.[2] Unfortunately, however, the surgery had an unseen and deadly consequence a short while later.

Brown wanted to continue on her travels. She planned to head to Panama next, and meet up with her fiancé James Stillman Rockefeller Jr, son of James Stillman Rockefeller Sr, the famed business magnate, Olympic rower, and—according to those with a preference for aluminium-based headwear—shadowy New World Order power-broker.[3] Brown was very keen to get over to Panama because it was there that she planned to marry Rockefeller and embark on their honeymoon.

The medical staff in charge of Brown, however, had other ideas. Brown had just gone through surgery, and she needed to rest and

---

2 Strictly speaking, she made it through in *two* pieces, once they'd taken out her appendix.

3 Despite a distinct lack of evidence, conspiracy theorists have never stopped believing that the Rockefeller family is behind a secretive, all-powerful world government. Then again, when has a distinct lack of evidence ever stopped conspiracy theorists from believing anything?

recuperate; she was in no fit state to go off globetrotting across the Atlantic. Brown disagreed, insisting that she was as fit as a fiddle. She offered a demonstration of just how healthy she was by energetically kicking up one of her legs, cancan style.

Sadly for Brown, this vigorous demonstration of her vitality ended up having the opposite result. Kicking her leg up dislodged a blood clot that was lurking after the surgery, and this blood clot promptly cut off the blood supply to her brain. This caused Brown to black out, and not long after this she was dead—before she even had a chance to bid the moon goodnight.

46

Gareth Jones

Died of a Heart Attack While Performing in a Play as a Character That Had a Heart Attack, 1958

There's method acting, such as when Daniel Day-Lewis caught pneumonia while filming *Gangs of New York* because he refused to wear modern, properly insulated clothing during the wintertime shoot, or when Jamie Foxx glued his eyelids shut to portray the blind Ray Charles in the film *Ray*. But then there's *method acting*, as once—and only once—demonstrated by Welsh actor Gareth Jones.

Jones was born in 1925, and after a brief stint at Aberystwyth University he decided to pursue the life of an actor, moving to London to study acting and seek the warm glow of the limelight. After relatively humble beginnings with a Scottish theatre group in Dundee, Jones began performing Shakespeare firstly in Stratford before making it all the way to London's West End, where he worked with a number of award-winning directors.

In London, Jones's career took off; by all accounts, he was headed for stardom. He was a talented actor, and his reputation as such only increased throughout the 1950s as he began to make regular appearances in plays performed for British television. Usually, these plays weren't pre-recorded, as they would be these days: they were performed live.

In 1958, an ITV program called *Armchair Theatre*, which featured live plays every week, was set to broadcast a play entitled *Underground* with Jones playing the character of Carl Norman. *Underground*, an adaptation of the Harold Rein novel *Few Were Left*, is about a group of people waiting for a train on the London Underground when an enormous explosion strikes the world aboveground, collapsing and blocking off the train tunnels; those who survived the blast underground have to come together and figure out what comes next. It sounds like a compelling bit of drama, but its performance on the evening of 30 November was overshadowed by some real-world drama that no one saw coming.

Before filming began, a fellow actor noticed that Jones wasn't in good nick, later commenting that he 'did not look well before we began. He was quiet, but I thought he was concentrating on his part.' But as Molière would tell us through a blood-soaked coughing fit, *the show must go on*—and so the broadcast of *Underground* went live, with Jones and the rest of the actors getting stuck into the first act.

During the second act, however, in the middle of a rushed make-up break for Jones while he was briefly off-camera, the ill-fated Welshman collapsed face-first into a make-up tray. The make-up artist summoned members of the crew and the on-site doctor, who quickly determined that Jones had suffered an instantly fatal heart attack on the make-up chair.

You can only imagine the confusion of the rest of the cast who, when Jones failed to return from his make-up break and take his position back on stage, were forced to ad-lib. 'Let's go down this tunnel,' one of the other actors quickly came up with. 'Carl must be waiting for us further down.'

Thoroughly bewildered and with no idea of what was going on, the cast bravely stuck the landing on the play's second act, and when the broadcast then went to a commercial break, they were gathered together by the director, Ted Kotcheff, for an explanation. Or a partial one, anyway.

Kotcheff decided that informing the cast of the death of one of their colleagues mid-show wouldn't be the best move because, again, *the show must go on*. He had spent the previous few minutes desperately scrambling to restructure the play and reassign all of Jones's lines to other characters to ensure that the whole thing still made sense, and so he just told the other actors that Jones was unwell and wouldn't be coming back on screen.

To their credit, the cast rose to the occasion and got through what would have been a very difficult third act, attempting to work around the absence of an important cast member while also probably feeling very anxious about his wellbeing. The crew faced similar challenges and ended up abandoning the camera script they'd been following. Instead, they improvised the switches between cameras and angles, ad-libbing in response to the ad-libs from the actors. It would have been a remarkable piece of television.[1]

Ultimately, the play was delivered as successfully as it possibly could have been under the circumstances. No perplexed viewers wrote in to complain; no one watching noticed anything too unusual. Critics panned the performance itself, calling it a little lifeless—and perhaps this was fair, if unknowingly tasteless, criticism.

After all, the play wouldn't have been helped by the fact that it was, necessarily, missing one of its most climactic scenes. Jones's absence, brought on by the fatal heart attack he had suffered, meant that this scene had to be omitted. It involved Jones's character, Carl, revealing himself as a traitor to the survivors and aligning himself instead with the play's antagonist, before suffering, believe it or not, a fatal heart attack.

In what is one of the most tragic[2] examples of method acting in the history of theatre, Jones died of a heart attack shortly before the character he played was scripted to meet the same fate. Never mind art imitating life; this was art imitating *death*.

---

1 Most unfortunately, no recording of the broadcast exists—back in 1958, they didn't record outgoing broadcasts as a matter of course as they do today.

2 And, admittedly, mistimed: Jones died of a heart attack during the second act, while his character wasn't actually supposed to do so until the third.

47

Prime Minister Harold Holt

Presumed Dead After Going Missing off the Coast, 1967

In 1966, Harold Holt became prime minister upon the retirement of Australia's longest-serving prime minister, Sir Robert Menzies.[1] Holt had big shoes to fill, but, happily, much of what he did while

1 Menzies was a red-blooded, freedom-loving PM who nonetheless had a somewhat selective approach to *what*, exactly, was to be free. Trade? Of course. Markets? Absolutely. Communists? I don't think so. Indigenous Australians? Certainly not.

prime minister helped to drag Australia, kicking and screaming, into the twentieth century—high time for such a thing, given it was the 1960s.

Holt played a huge part in moving Australia away from the reprehensible White Australia policy, a racist immigration policy that heavily restricted non-white migrants from entering Australia. Despite being a member of Australia's conservative political party,[2] Holt undid much of the White Australia policy, and in doing so paved the way for a better Australia. His political legacy was also further bolstered by him overseeing constitutional reform that offered some recognition to Indigenous Australians.

That's not to say Holt was perfect—far from it, in fact. For instance, he aligned himself very closely with the disastrous foreign policy of US president Lyndon B. Johnson and his efforts in Vietnam. This didn't sit well with Australians, but like it or not our boys were conscripted and shipped off to fight in Vietnam, tarnishing Holt's record as prime minister.

However, the most remarkable thing about Holt's prime ministership is how it ended: with his presumed death in late 1967, at which point he hadn't even been prime minister for two years.

Holt was a keen swimmer. He loved the ocean, he liked to go swimming and spearfishing, and he even had a little coastal holiday home down in Portsea, at the southern end of Port Phillip Bay, not far from the Victorian capital city of Melbourne. In December 1967,

2 The very unhelpfully named Liberal Party.

he was staying at his holiday home with some of his friends, and it was on this trip that his life—we assume—came to a premature end.

On 17 December 1967, while cutting about with his mates down around Point Nepean, Holt made a stop at Cheviot Beach, where he'd swum many times before. He fancied a dip, although the surf that day was very rough. Not liking the look of the water, most of the people he was with decided not to go in; only one of them, a man named Alan Stewart, joined Holt for a swim.

Stewart wasn't taking any chances with the rough conditions and stuck close to the shore. On the other hand, Holt, who claimed to 'know this beach like the back of my hand', was much more confident and headed out further into the surf. Before long, he was caught up in a strong rip: a fast-moving current of water that can quickly pull swimmers away from the shore. As any beach-going reader will know, rips can be very dangerous; they're a leading cause of drowning at beaches worldwide.

This rip took hold of Holt and dragged him further and further out, past the breakers and out of sight of his mates on shore. To this day, this remains somewhat perplexing: Holt was an experienced swimmer, and despite being 59, was in decent physical shape. Consequently, he would have known how to deal with a rip,[3] so the fact that he let this one sweep him away is a mystery.

3 Don't swim against the current, back towards the shore; instead, swim sideways, parallel to the shore, out of the current's pull. Learning this is the easy part—*remembering* it while panicking about being dragged out into the open ocean is another thing entirely.

In any case, once his friends realised that Holt had been taken by this rip, they got into gear and called the authorities. Within an hour, a huge search party was underway, seeking any sign whatsoever of the missing prime minister.

Helicopters and boats scoured the nearby sea for Holt, while divers went out into the water at Cheviot Beach to search beneath the surface, but the conditions were so rough that they had a very hard time of it and many had to come back ashore. Unfortunately, bad weather hampered the search for the next three days; in the end, no sign of him was found.

The search was officially abandoned on 5 January 1968. Harold Holt had disappeared without a trace, never to be seen again.

Of course, all of the usual whackos enthusiastically put on their tinfoil hats and came out of the woodwork to put forward conspiracy theories: the CIA had killed Holt because he wanted to withdraw Australian troops from Vietnam, he had defected to China and was picked up by one of their submarines, he had faked his own death to elope with a lover; there were all sorts of marvellous conjectures. And all of them were nonsense, of course. There wasn't—and still isn't—a shred of evidence to support any of these absurd theories. Holt's death was just a tragic accident that highlights the dangers of rip currents when swimming in the ocean.

But we haven't yet come to the best part of the story about Holt's unfortunate demise—that part came *after* his death.

The strange and mysterious death of a national head of government brought about memorial services and commemorations throughout not just Australia but also the world. Additionally, as you might expect, plenty of stuff in Australia was named after him following his passing: there's a suburb in Canberra called Holt, as well as some fishing reserves in Victoria; even a US warship was named in his honour, the USS *Harold E. Holt*.

However, of all the stuff that was named after Harold Holt, nothing is funnier than what happened with a local government project in his electorate, in the Melbourne suburb of Glen Iris.

At the time of Holt's death, the local council was overseeing some renovations to a recreational complex in Glen Iris that was in need of work. Therefore, given the circumstances, the Malvern City Council announced that they were renaming this complex after the former PM. As a way to honour Holt after his unexpected and untimely end, it was a thoughtful and touching decision, you'd think.

And it *would* have been, were it not for the nature of this particular government complex that was under renovation.

Today you can head out to High Street in Glen Iris, on the 6 tram, and visit this complex, named in the wake of the disappearance and presumed drowning death of an Australian prime minister. In what is probably the most hilarious local government decision history has ever seen, the Malvern City Council decided to name a *pool complex* after the bloke: the Harold Holt Memorial Swimming Centre.

48

Sir Billy Snedden

Died 'on the Job', 1987

Harold Holt isn't the only Australian politician to have died in bizarre circumstances. While he never made it to the office of prime minister, Sir Billy Snedden was another senior figure in Australia's Liberal Party whose death made more than a few headlines. Although, rather than involving a mysterious disappearance at sea, these headlines instead involved Snedden, his son, and his son's ex-lover. No, don't bother getting your mind out of the gutter—your salacious guesses at the circumstances surrounding Snedden's death are probably more correct than you realise.

Snedden was born in 1926, the son of Scottish immigrants whose healthy British suspicion of all things foreign meant that they moved from a town near Perth in Scotland to a town near Perth in Australia, just to be safe. Snedden scraped through a law degree and then partook in a traditional hobby of Perth locals when in 1954 he left Perth and moved to Melbourne. There, after a brief stint as a lawyer, he stood as a Liberal candidate and was elected to federal parliament, working in the government of Australia's longest-serving prime minister, Sir Robert Menzies.

Snedden also served under prime ministers Harold Holt, John McEwen,[1] John Gorton, and William McMahon, and he held portfolios such as Minister for Immigration, and Minister for Labour and National Service. This latter position gave him the unenviable job of having to defend Australia's ongoing and immensely unpopular conscription policies, which he did with exceptional poise and eloquence when he described anti-war protesters as 'political bikies pack-raping democracy'.

In 1972, the McMahon government was booted out by Labor's Gough Whitlam, who ended 23 years of successive conservative governments with a campaign based on the provision of universal health care, the removal of university fees and, seemingly, the assertion of the importance of punctuality with the election slogan 'It's Time'. After Whitlam's win, Snedden became Leader of the Opposition, but he wasn't very good at it—a fact highlighted during the 1974 election,

1 Who, with only 22 days in office, hardly counts.

when Whitlam's Labor Party left behind the punchy and iconic approach to election slogans that brought us 'It's Time', and instead ran with the somewhat less sophisticated 'I'm dreadin' Snedden'.[2]

Snedden and the Liberals lost, although not according to Snedden. In a post-election press conference, Snedden insisted 'we were not defeated. We did not win enough seats in order to form a government.' In a broadly two-party system like Australia's, it's not immediately clear what the difference is, but according to Snedden there was some sort of important distinction that most were missing.

In any case, Snedden went on to lose the leadership of the Liberal Party in 1975 to future Liberal prime minister Malcolm Fraser, and given Snedden's overall ineffectiveness and inability to articulate even the most basic messages appropriately, he was perfectly suited for the office of Speaker of the House. Shortly after the Liberals returned to government, Snedden served as Speaker from 1976 until Labor returned to power in 1983 under Bob Hawke.[3] Snedden then resigned

---

2 This isn't a joke: it was a real political campaign slogan used by Labor supporters in 1974. As ridiculous as it sounds, it's certainly a breath of fresh air compared to the usual uninspired nonsense that is wheeled out by parties across the political spectrum every election season: 'We'll Put People First', 'Stand Up For Real Action', etc. As truly unpleasant as former Labor leader Mark Latham has become in more recent years, he did give us a great gift in 2004 with the incredible slogan 'Ease the Squeeze'.

3 Hawke is said to have held a world record for sculling a yard (1.4 litres) of beer in eleven seconds. This record has been called into question in recent years, however, with claims that it was fabricated to make Hawke more appealing to Australian voters. If this is so, based on the general state of the average Australian voter, and based on the fact that Hawke still holds the all-time record for an Australian PM's approval rating, it's fair to say it worked.

from parliament but evidently wasn't yet ready to stop spending his time surrounded by loud and entitled rich people, as he served as the chairman of the Melbourne Football Club until 1986.

In 1987, however, Snedden's life came to an abrupt end in a Sydney Travelodge at the age of just 60. Just a few hours after attending future Liberal prime minister John Howard's campaign launch, Snedden returned to his hotel and died of a heart attack while sharing what could delicately be described as *vigorous bipartisan negotiations* with a younger woman known only as Wendy.

Well, actually, no—she wasn't *only* known as Wendy. She was also known as the former lover of Snedden's own son: Snedden died while shagging his son's ex. Hilariously, by all accounts this came as no surprise to his very understanding son, who knew that his old man had an appetite for enjoying extracurricular social activities.

The media was all over Snedden's scandalous departure from this mortal coil. In the wake of Snedden's remarkable death, one newspaper ran with the tremendous headline 'SNEDDEN "DIED ON THE JOB"', while another diligently assured readers that the contraceptive precaution that Snedden used had indeed fulfilled its function, from start to finish. Thus, not only did Snedden die doing what he loved, it also seems that he was coming as he was going.

49

Cachi the Poodle, Marta Espina, Edith Solá, and an Unknown Man

Fell from a Tall Building, Killed by a Falling Dog, Hit by a Bus After Seeing Someone Get Killed by a Falling Dog, and Had a Heart Attack After Seeing Someone Get Killed by a Falling Dog and Someone Else Get Hit by a Bus, Respectively, 1988

On 21 October 1988, on the thirteenth floor of an apartment building above a busy street in the Argentinian capital of Buenos Aires, a small poodle named Cachi left behind a life of tranquil domesticity and instead very briefly took up the life of a canine skydiver. For reasons that still remain unclear, Cachi hurtled off a balcony high above the ground and plunged towards the pavement below at a velocity that would prove to be terminal in every sense of the word.

Good news for dog lovers: Cachi never actually hit the pavement. Bad news for old lady lovers:[1] the dog's fall was broken by a 75-year-old woman named Marta Espina. Both Cachi and Espina were killed instantly; while poodles aren't generally considered among the deadliest of the dog breeds, it turns out that the only thing they've been missing in order to earn a place alongside pit bull terriers and the Presa Canarios on governmental Dangerous and Menacing Dog Breed lists is the meteoric speed that comes with throwing yourself off the thirteenth floor.

It's fair to say that an Argentinian septuagenarian being slain by a falling poodle might have been enough in its own right for a chapter in this book, albeit a very short one. Cachi's fall, however, would end up being far deadlier.

After Cachi's murderous descent, a stunned crowd began to converge around the crumpled bodies, both human and canine, beneath the apartment building. Quite a large crowd, it seems, because as more and more curious onlookers approached to have a good old

1 Not like *that*. Unless . . .

stickybeak, people ended up spilling out from the footpath and onto the street. This was bad news for one stickybeak in particular, a woman named Edith Solá. In the middle of the street itself—perhaps as she was crossing over to get a better look at what had happened—Solá was hit by a passing bus and died instantly.

Just imagine what this would have been like for the crowd of onlookers: firstly, a dog falls out of the sky and kills an old lady; then, as people hurry over to see what had happened and lend assistance, a bus cleans up someone else. Even the sternest constitution would be tested, and in the case of one poor man whose name didn't make it into the papers, it was a test he failed.

An unidentified man reportedly suffered a heart attack after witnessing these cascading deaths, and he subsequently decided to throw his hat into the ring along with them. After seeing him collapse to the ground, the crowd called an ambulance, but it was no good. The man died on the way to hospital, bringing Cachi's kill-to-death ratio all the way up to 3:1—more impressive than even the world's best professional Counter-Strike players.

50

Garry Hoy

Died while Demonstrating Just How Tough the Glass in a Skyscraper's Windows Was, 1993

Garry Hoy was a Canadian lawyer who died in 1993 . . .

Wait, 1993? A *history* book is hardly the place for something that happened so recently, surely. Why, it wasn't all that long ago that we were watching *Jurassic Park* and listening to *Whoomp! (There It Is)* by Tag Team, cutting about in baggy flannel shirts and Air Jordan VIIIs. Right, everyone? *Right?*

A gentle reminder, dear reader, that 1993 was *over 30 years ago.*

Yes, you're that old. *Shrek* was released two decades ago; new episodes of *Seinfeld* haven't been aired for a quarter of a century.

Your knees will make those exciting crunchy noises for the rest of your life, and your doctor does kind of have a point about your cholesterol levels.

This is a book about death. What did you expect, to be made to feel young and immortal?

Anyway—we're going all the way back here, through the depths of history, to the ancient and forgotten days of the late second millennium CE: to 1993, the year that saw the death of Garry Hoy. Hoy worked for the Toronto law firm Holden Day Wilson, and had a little party trick he loved to pull off to entertain the firm's newest employees.

The offices of Holden Day Wilson were on the 24th floor of a Torontonian skyscraper, with magnificently impressive floor-to-ceiling windows affording a spectacular view of the surrounding city. And, for some reason, while taking new hires on a tour of the offices, Hoy liked to personally demonstrate the tensile strength of the glass in these giant windows by running and hurling himself at them at full tilt.

Every time he did this,[1] he would bounce off harmlessly, and the new employees would be . . . impressed, presumably? They'd all pull out their brick-like Ericsson EH237 mobile phones from the pockets of their high-waisted baggy suit pants and call a friend to tell them what they'd just seen, describing the demonstration as perhaps hella fly, or even majorly dope.[2]

1 Well, every time except one.

2 You can hang shit on Gen Z for a lot of different things, but even their impenetrable slang isn't as truly ludicrous as the nonsense Gen X came up with.

It remains uncertain as to exactly why Hoy was obsessed with demonstrating how tough the windowpanes were when onboarding new employees. Maybe it was machismo and bravado, or maybe he just had a strong interest in structural engineering and wanted to share his passion. Whatever the case, in seeking to demonstrate to everyone just how strong these sheets of glass were, he really did prove his point in the most emphatic way possible.

On 9 July 1993, Garry Hoy rammed himself, for the very last time, into a windowpane on the 24th floor of this skyscraper. He was absolutely right about the tensile strength of this glass. It didn't break.

But the frame sure as hell did! The glass, still intact, *burst out of its frame*, and you can only imagine Hoy's very brief surprise as he hurtled down to the pavement below.

After the inquest into this tragic incident, Hoy's death was filed under the category of 'accidental auto-defenestration'. Presumably, they would have had to label a new folder for the paperwork.

Meanwhile, Holden Day Wilson was overflowing with tributes for poor Hoy, describing him as 'one of the best and brightest'. Which is perhaps fair to call into question, given one aspect of his behaviours while at the company—but then again, the firm shut down three years later, so maybe he really was essential. This does make sense, from a certain perspective, because if there's one way to accurately describe Garry Hoy, it certainly would be as a high-flying lawyer.

Acknowledgements

This book wouldn't have been possible without the enormous amount of work that was done by people who are all tremendously more competent and capable than I am. First and foremost, to the team at Allen & Unwin, in particular my publisher Sally Heath and editor Sam Kent: thank you for your endless expertise in helping me make this book the best it possibly could be. I'm especially grateful to Sally for taking a punt on a brand-new author.

To the vigilant and incisive Dannielle Viera, who edited this book's manuscript: thank you for your uncompromising work in ensuring my writing was presented consistently and correctly. This book was improved immeasurably through your insight, accuracy, and rigour—even if we don't quite see eye to eye on the Oxford comma.

To the meticulous and keen-eyed Brooke Lyons, who proofread this book: thank you for correcting all the small errors I made, from the misplaced commas to the missing diacritics. I'm still in awe of your attention to detail, and still slightly embarrassed by just how many mistakes you managed to find.

To the immensely talented Andrew Foxglove, who provided the illustration found on the front cover: thank you for creating such a magnificent piece of art for this book. They say not to judge a book by its cover, but I do hope that people judge this one based specifically on what you drew.

To the team at WME, in particular my agents Florence Dodd and Alex Bewley: thank you for getting me my first publishing deal, and for your near-infinite patience when it comes to my hopeless inexperience. I greatly appreciate all your help with making the leap from being a tinpot podcaster to being a tinpot author.

To the team at Acast, in particular Ryan Lamont and Simon McDermott: thank you for making sure that my podcast, *Half-Arsed History*, appears in listeners' feeds every week, and for helping me to build my career as a podcaster with all your advice and assistance.

To the team at SquareSound, in particular Keenan Wardrope and Justine Sloane-Lees: thank you for all your help in producing the audiobook version of *History's Strangest Deaths*. One might think all my years of podcasting would make recording an audiobook a relatively simple affair—and one would be very wrong. I appreciate your excellent direction and boundless forbearance.

To Prithi Dey at Spotify, where *Half-Arsed History* stopped being a hobby and started being a career: thank you for seeing something in my work that I didn't ever really see myself.

To Rich Hagon and Greg Collins, two people who have done

more for my career over the years than I think even they realise: thank you for the decade or more of belief, backing, and opportunity.

To Roger Clarke: thank you for the unceasing guidance and support, professionally and personally, and for sharing a great love of history with me. It's been a very interesting journey over the years; I want to thank you for coming.

To the teachers who developed and influenced my writing, from Anne Gillard in Year 7 to Sam Bryant in Year 12: thank you for all the advice, criticism, and red pen. So much of what you taught me is with me still. A special thank you goes to Rodney Smith, whose teaching helped awaken my passion for the stories of the past. I should also acknowledge my Year 11 history teacher, Richard Wakeham, who awarded me a failing grade and characterised my work as 'a series of unsubstantiated generalisations with no evidence'. Two decades later, nothing has changed.

And to the listeners of *Half-Arsed History*: thank you for being there, week in and week out, listening to my silly nonsense, emailing in topic suggestions and feedback, and helping to grow the show to what it is today by telling your friends, your enemies, and the people about whom you feel largely ambivalent. I know that I tell you this every single week, but it really is great to have you along.

There are so many creators who have had a huge influence on me and my work over the years. None of the stuff I make would be what it is without the writers, comedians, musicians, podcasters, artists, and other exceptionally gifted people whose work I admire so greatly: John Darnielle, Ben Gibbard, John Linnell and John Flansburgh,

Hamish Blake and Andy Lee, Shaun Micallef, Terry Pratchett, Bill Bryson, David Hunt, Sid Meier, Amir Rao and Gavin Simon, Lukas Pope, and so many others. They don't know who I am or what I do, but I am who I am and I do what I do because of them.

My parents, Loretta and Martin, cultivated within me a deep love for reading and writing from the earliest age, and for that I am immensely grateful. Thank you so very much, Mum and Dad—I never dreamed that I would one day become a published author, and I couldn't have done it without the two of you. Obviously. I couldn't have done very much *at all* without the two of you, I suppose.

But my most profound debt of gratitude goes to the woman who will, shortly after this book's publication, become my wife:[1] Megan, whose unyielding belief in me and my writing is the foundational reason that this book was transformed from an abstract idea into an actual, real, tangible thing. Thank you, mate, for everything.

Finally, thank you to my little cat, Scotia, whose eternal indifference outshines the sun. I definitely *could* have done it without her, but I'm glad I didn't have to.

---

1 Hopefully, anyway. She still has a few weeks to come to her senses, although by now it's far too late to get back all the deposits.